WHAT IS THE BOOK OF ECCLESIASTES?

Kids' Guides to God's Word Series

What Is the Book of Genesis?
What Is the Book of Exodus?
What Is the Book of Leviticus?
What Is the Book of Numbers?
What Is the Book of Deuteronomy?
What Is the Book of Joshua?
What Is the Book of Judges?
What Is the Book of Ruth?
What Is the Book of 1 Samuel?
What Is the Book of 2 Samuel?
What Is the Book of 1 Kings?
What Is the Book of 2 Kings?
What Are the Books of 1–2 Chronicles?
What Are the Books of Ezra & Nehemiah?
What Is the Book of Esther?
What Is the Book of Job?
What Is the Book of Psalms?
What Is the Book of Proverbs?
What Is the Book of Ecclesiastes?
What Are the Books of Song of Songs & Lamentations?
What Is the Book of Isaiah?
What Is the Book of Jeremiah?
What Is the Book of Ezekiel?
What Is the Book of Daniel?
What Are the Books of Hosea–Micah?
What Are the Books of Nahum–Malachi?

What Is the Gospel of Matthew?
What Is the Gospel of Mark?
What Is the Gospel of Luke?
What Is the Gospel of John?
What Is the Book of Acts?
What Is the Book of Romans?
What Is the Book of 1 Corinthians?
What Is the Book of 2 Corinthians?
What Is the Book of Galatians?
What Is the Book of Ephesians?
What Is the Book of Philippians?
What Are the Books of Colossians & Philemon?
What Are the Books of 1–2 Thessalonians?
What Are the Books of 1–2 Timothy & Titus?
What Is the Book of Hebrews?
What Is the Book of James?
What Are the Books of 1–2 Peter & Jude?
What Are the Books of 1–3 John?
What Is the Book of Revelation?

What Is the Book of

ECCLESIASTES?

Michael Whitworth

ISBN 978-1-971767-05-5

Published by Start2Finish
Bend, Oregon 97702
start2finish.org

Printed in the United States of America
30 29 28 27 26   1 2 3 4 5

CONTENTS

INTRODUCTION

Have you ever worked really hard on something—a project, a game, a goal—and when you finally got it, you thought, "That's it? I thought I'd feel... *more*."

Maybe you saved up for something you wanted, and a week later it was just another thing in your room. Maybe you got the grade or made the team or hit the level in a video game, and the excitement wore off before dinner. That weird, empty feeling isn't a sign something's wrong with you. It's actually what an entire book of the Bible is about.

The book is called Ecclesiastes, and it was written by a guy called "the Teacher." And he starts with a line that sounds super depressing: "Everything is meaningless" (Ecclesiastes 1:2).

Wait—what? Isn't the Bible supposed to be encouraging?

Here's the thing: the Teacher isn't saying life is pointless. He's saying that chasing after stuff to make you happy is like trying to catch fog or smoke. You can see it. You can reach for it. But every time you grab, your hand comes up empty.

The Teacher was a king. He had money, power, and time to try everything. Parties. Projects. Building cool stuff. Getting super smart. And you know what he said after doing it all? It was "like chasing the wind" (Ecclesiastes 2:11). None of it filled him up the way he thought it would.

This might sound like a bummer, but it's actually really helpful—because it tells you the truth that a lot of people don't figure out until they're way older: **You can't find the meaning of life by collecting achievements or stuff.**

The world tries to sell you a different story. Social media is full of people showing off their "best life." Influencers promise that if you just do this one thing, you'll be happy. Adults stress about promotions and houses and vacations like those things will finally make everything okay. But the Teacher says: "Been there, done that, still felt empty."

So what's the point?

Here's where Ecclesiastes gets surprisingly good. The Teacher doesn't just complain—he gives you a different way to live. Instead of chasing things that don't last, he says to receive what God gives. Pay attention to the simple stuff. A good meal with your family. A rest day after hard work. Laughing with your friends. These aren't just random nice moments—they're gifts from God.

The Teacher says five times in the book to "eat, drink, and enjoy your life." Not because life is perfect, but because God is good—and learning to notice his gifts is way better than always grabbing for the next thing.

There's something else the Teacher says over and over: "Fear God." That doesn't mean be scared of him. It means remember that he's God and you're not. Stop trying to control everything. Stop acting like you can figure out the whole universe. Trust that God knows what he's doing, even when life doesn't make sense.

And here's the coolest part: Ecclesiastes points straight to Jesus. The Teacher says life under the sun is short and confusing—and he's right. But the God who lives in heaven didn't leave us alone down here. He came. Jesus stepped into our messy, confusing world. He experienced everything we experience—including death. And then he beat it. Ecclesiastes says everything fades like smoke. Jesus says, "I make all things new."

So why should you care about this ancient book? Because you're going to hear a million voices telling you that happiness is just one more achievement away. One more social media follower. One more win. One more vacation. One more thing. And Ecclesiastes says, "Don't fall for it." That's not where life is found.

Real life is found in trusting God, enjoying what he gives you *today*, and knowing that even when things don't make sense, you're not in charge—and that's actually good news.

You don't have to figure everything out. You don't have to win at life. You just have to receive it.

So next time you feel that weird emptiness after getting something you wanted, remember: You're not broken. You're just learning what the Teacher learned thousands of years ago.

Everything fades like smoke.

But every good gift? That's God saying, "I see you. I'm here. And you're mine."

1

RUNNING ON A TREADMILL TO NOWHERE

Have you ever been on a treadmill? You can run for miles and never actually go anywhere. Your legs are pumping, your heart is racing, sweat is dripping down your face—and you're staring at the exact same spot on the wall the whole time. The machine tells you how far you've "gone," but when you step off, you're in the exact same place you started.

That's basically how the book of Ecclesiastes begins.

The writer—we call him "the Teacher" or "the Preacher"—looks out at the world and sees something that might surprise you: Everyone is running on a treadmill. We go to school, do our homework, try to get good grades, try to impress people, try to level up, try to get the next thing—and we never quite arrive anywhere that feels like *enough*. We're always chasing something.

The Teacher asks a question that might keep you up at night if you think about it too long: "What does anyone really gain from all their hard work?" (Ecclesiastes 1:3).

It's not that work is bad. It's not that trying hard is pointless. But the Teacher wants us to stop and wonder: Does all this effort actually get us somewhere meaningful? Or are we just running in place?

THE WORD THAT CHANGES EVERYTHING

Before we go further, you need to know one Hebrew word: *hebel* (pronounced *HEH-bell*). It's the most important word in the whole book. Most Bibles translate it as "meaningless" or "vanity," but that's not quite right. *Hebel* literally means "breath" or "vapor." You know when it's really cold outside and you breathe out and see that little cloud? That's *hebel*. It's real— you can see it. But a second later? Gone. You can't grab it. You can't keep it. It just... disappears.

That's what the Teacher says life is like. "Everything is *hebel*," he says right at the beginning (1:2). Everything is like breath on a cold day. Real, but impossible to hold onto. Beautiful, but temporary.

Now, here's the important part: The Teacher isn't saying life is silly or worthless. He's saying life is *fragile*. It slips through your fingers. You can't control it. And if you spend your whole life trying to grab onto things that disappear—popularity, achievements, stuff—you're going to end up exhausted and confused.

Put the treadmill and the breath together, and you've got Ecclesiastes 1. We run hard. We work hard. We chase hard. And what we catch? It vanishes like mist.

THE SUN, THE WIND, AND THE RIVERS

The Teacher does something really cool in this chapter. He looks at nature to show us what he means.

First, the sun: "The sun rises and the sun sets, then hurries around to rise again" (1:5). Every single day, the sun does its job. Rise. Set. Rise. Set. It never takes a break. It never does anything different. And yet—has anything really changed? Tomorrow will look pretty much like today.

Then, the wind: "The wind blows south, and then turns north. Around and around it goes, blowing in circles" (1:6). The wind moves constantly, but it doesn't get anywhere. It just keeps spinning in circles.

Finally, the rivers: "All the rivers flow to the sea, but the sea never becomes full" (1:7). Think about that. Every river on earth is pouring water into the ocean, all day, every day. And the ocean is *still not full*. The cycle just keeps going.

The Teacher isn't saying nature is boring. He's making a point: The world keeps spinning, keeps repeating, keeps cycling—and it doesn't seem to be heading toward some big finish line. The sun doesn't retire. The wind doesn't stop. The ocean doesn't fill up and say, "Okay, I'm done."

And here's the uncomfortable part: *We're kind of the same.*

Generations come and go. Your great-great-great-grandparents lived and worked and worried about stuff—and most of us don't even know their names. One day, people won't remember us either. The Teacher isn't trying to be mean about this. He's just being honest. Human memory is short. Time marches on. The world keeps spinning whether we're here or not.

WHY WE'RE NEVER SATISFIED

Here's a question: Have you ever gotten something you really wanted—and then felt kind of... empty afterward?

Maybe it was a video game you saved up for. You were so excited. You finally got it. You played it for a week. And then... it was just another game. The excitement wore off, and you started wanting the next thing.

The Teacher totally gets this. "No matter how much we see, we are never satisfied. No matter how much we hear, we are not content" (1:8). In other words, you can watch a million videos, scroll through infinite feeds, listen to endless music— and you'll still want more. You'll never reach a point where you say, "Okay, I've seen everything. I'm satisfied forever now."

That's not because something is wrong with you. That's because nothing in this world was designed to fully satisfy you. The Teacher is naming something every human being eventually feels: the ache for more that nothing earthly can fill.

It's like having a cup with a tiny hole in the bottom. You keep pouring stuff in—experiences, achievements, stuff—but it keeps leaking out. You never feel full for long.

NOTHING NEW UNDER THE SUN

One of the most famous lines in Ecclesiastes is this: "There is nothing new under the sun" (1:9).

Wait—what about smartphones? Space travel? TikTok? Those are new, right?

Well, kind of. The technology is new. But the people using it? We're pretty much the same as humans have always been. We still get jealous. We still want to be liked. We still worry about the future. We still fight over dumb stuff. We still search for meaning.

Every generation thinks they're living in the most important, most unique moment in history. And in some ways, they are. But the Teacher says the human heart doesn't really change. We keep reinventing the outside—new gadgets, new styles, new trends—but inside, we're running the same old patterns our ancestors ran.

That's not depressing; it's actually freeing. It means you don't have to pressure yourself to be "unique" in some world-changing way. You're part of a long, long line of humans who've all struggled with the same questions. You're not alone.

THE PART ABOUT BEING FORGOTTEN

Here's the hardest verse in the chapter: "We don't remember what happened in the past, and in future generations, no one will remember what we are doing now" (1:11).

Ouch.

The Teacher is saying that even the most famous people eventually fade from memory. Think about it—there were kings and queens and warriors and geniuses who lived thousands of years ago, and nobody today knows their names. In a few hundred years, the celebrities and athletes and influencers we obsess over now will probably be forgotten too.

So why does the Teacher bring this up? Because he wants to free us from the pressure of being remembered. If the whole point of your life is to be famous, to leave a legacy, to have your name live on forever—well, history says that's probably not going to work out. The world forgets.

But here's the thing the Teacher hints at but doesn't fully explain yet: God doesn't forget. Human memory is short. But God's memory is eternal. He remembers every person, every moment, every act of faithfulness—even the stuff nobody else ever sees. If the only memory that really matters is God's, then we can stop frantically trying to make ourselves unforgettable. We can just live faithfully, knowing we're seen and known by the One whose memory never fades.

SO WHAT'S THE POINT?

By now you might be thinking, "This is kind of a bummer, isn't it?" But the Teacher isn't trying to make you sad. He's trying to make you free.

See, most people spend their lives running on the treadmill, believing that if they just run a little faster, try a little harder, get a little more—they'll finally arrive somewhere satisfying. The Teacher says, "Stop. The treadmill doesn't lead anywhere."

That's not bad news. That's honest news. And once you stop expecting the treadmill to take you somewhere it can't, you can finally start looking for meaning in the right place.

Life is *hebel*—breath, vapor, mist. But here's what's amazing: God is the one who breathed that breath into you in the first place. The same God who made the sun rise and the wind blow and the rivers flow also made you. And he didn't make you to run on a treadmill forever. He made you to know him.

The stuff you chase—grades, likes, achievements, popularity—those aren't bad things. But they're vapor. They disappear. And if you build your whole life on vapor, you'll always feel like you're grasping at air.

But if you build your life on God—the One who made you, sees you, and remembers you forever—then even the vapor starts to make sense. The small moments become gifts. The ordinary days become meaningful. The breath that disappears becomes a reminder that every single one of them came from him.

WHAT THIS MEANS FOR YOU

The Teacher isn't telling you to stop trying. He's not saying school doesn't matter or hard work is pointless. He's saying, "Don't expect those things to give you what only God can give."

Work hard, but don't worship success.

Enjoy good things, but don't expect them to satisfy you forever.

Pay attention to the small gifts—a good meal, a fun day with friends, a moment when you actually feel peaceful—because those are signs of God's goodness.

And when you feel that weird ache, that restless sense that something's missing, don't panic. That's not a bug; it's a feature. You were made for more than this world can offer. That ache is pointing you somewhere.

Ecclesiastes 1 is like the first step in a long journey. The Teacher clears away all the lies we believe—that stuff will satisfy us, that achievements will complete us, that being remembered will make us matter. He strips all that away so we can finally see the truth.

Life is breath. Life is vapor. But vapor breathed out by God? That's something worth paying attention to.

So the next time you feel like you're running on a treadmill to nowhere—stop. Step off. Take a breath. And remember: The God who made you hasn't forgotten you.

Even when the vapor fades, God remains.

2

THE KING WHO HAD EVERYTHING

Imagine the richest person you can think of. Maybe it's a tech billionaire with a private jet and a house the size of a shopping mall. Maybe it's a famous YouTuber with millions of subscribers and brand deals coming out of their ears. Maybe it's a pro athlete who's won every championship and has a trophy room bigger than your entire home.

Now imagine that person lying in bed at night, staring at the ceiling, thinking, "Why do I still feel empty?"

That's basically the story of Ecclesiastes 1:12–2:26.

The Teacher wasn't just some random guy giving advice. He was a king. His name was Solomon, the wealthiest and wisest king Israel ever had. This guy had *everything*. Palaces. Gardens. Servants. Gold. Music. Entertainment. Literally anything he wanted, he could have.

And he decided to run an experiment: "Can any of this stuff actually make me happy?"

Spoiler alert: It didn't.

THE EXPERIMENT BEGINS

The Teacher starts by telling us he wasn't just dabbling in this stuff. He went all in. "I applied my heart to seek and search out by wisdom all that is done under heaven" (1:13). He wasn't scrolling casually through life. He was doing serious research—studying, observing, trying to figure out how the world works and whether any of it could give him lasting satisfaction.

His first experiment? Wisdom.

Makes sense, right? If you're smart enough, you can figure out life. You can avoid mistakes, make good decisions, and find the secret to happiness. So the Teacher became the wisest person around. He studied everything. He understood more than anyone before him.

And you know what he discovered? "In much wisdom is much vexation, and he who increases knowledge increases sorrow" (1:18).

Wait—what? Being smart makes you *sadder*?

Here's what he means: The more you understand about the world, the more you see what's broken. The more you learn, the more problems you notice. Wisdom is like turning on a bright light in a messy room—suddenly you see all the dust and clutter you didn't notice before. Understanding doesn't fix the mess; it just helps you see it more clearly.

Wisdom is good. But it can't carry the weight of your whole life.

MAYBE FUN IS THE ANSWER?

So the Teacher pivots. If wisdom doesn't work, maybe pleasure will. "I said in my heart, 'Come now, I will test you with pleasure; enjoy yourself'" (2:1). He throws himself into entertainment, laughter, parties, good food, good drink—basically anything that feels good. If life is hard, maybe the secret is just to have as much fun as possible.

But here's what he found: "I said of laughter, 'It is mad,' and of pleasure, 'What use is it?'" (2:2). Fun is... fun. But it doesn't last. The party ends. The laughs fade. The next morning, you wake up and nothing has really changed. Entertainment can distract you for a while, but it can't fill the hole inside you.

Think about it: Have you ever binged a show you loved, finished the last episode, and felt kind of sad afterward? That's what the Teacher is talking about. Pleasure is like cotton candy—it tastes great for a second, then it's gone, and you're left wanting something more.

WHAT ABOUT BUILDING STUFF?

Okay, so wisdom didn't work. Pleasure didn't work. What about achievement? The Teacher goes full construction mode: "I built houses and planted vineyards for myself. I made myself gardens and parks... I made myself pools... I bought male and female servants... I had also great possessions of herds and flocks... I also gathered for myself silver and gold and the treasure of kings" (2:4–8).

This guy built an empire. Houses, gardens, pools, farms, art collections, musicians, wealth beyond imagination. He didn't just succeed—he dominated. If success could make someone happy, the Teacher should have been the happiest person alive.

And for a while, he enjoyed it. "My heart found pleasure in all my toil" (2:10). The work itself felt good. Building stuff is satisfying. Accomplishing goals gives you a rush.

But then came the crash: "Then I considered all that my hands had done and the toil I had expended in doing it, and behold, all was vanity and a striving after wind, and there was nothing to be gained under the sun" (2:11). After all that work, all that success, all that building—he looked around and thought, "What did I actually gain?"

The projects were impressive. But they didn't last forever. The pleasure faded. The achievements couldn't stop time. He still got older. He still felt empty. The treadmill kept spinning.

THE PROBLEM WITH LEAVING STUFF BEHIND

Here's where the Teacher gets really honest—and kind of sad. "I hated all my toil in which I toil under the sun, seeing that I must leave it to the man who will come after me" (2:18). Think about that. You spend your whole life building something—working hard, sacrificing, creating—and then you die and hand it off to someone else. And that person might be wise... or they might be a complete fool who wastes everything you built.

You don't get to control what happens to your stuff after you're gone. You don't get to guarantee your legacy. Someone else inherits everything, and they'll do whatever they want with it. That's a hard pill to swallow when you've poured your life into something.

The Teacher says this realization made him despair. Not because he was lazy or ungrateful—but because he was honest. If all your work ends up in someone else's hands, and you can't control what they do with it, then what's the point of working so hard in the first place?

WAIT—THERE'S HOPE?

Right when everything seems totally depressing, the Teacher makes a surprising turn. "There is nothing better for a person than that he should eat and drink and find enjoyment in his toil. This also, I saw, is from the hand of God" (2:24).

Hold on—didn't he just say pleasure was empty? Didn't he just say work was pointless?

Here's the difference: The Teacher isn't saying pleasure and work are bad. He's saying they can't carry the weight of your whole life. They're not designed to give you ultimate meaning. But when you receive them as gifts from God, they become something different.

See, the problem isn't enjoying a good meal or feeling satisfied after hard work. The problem is expecting those things to fill your soul. When you demand that food or success or entertainment make you happy forever, they'll always disappoint you. But when you receive them as small gifts from a generous God? They become beautiful. "For apart from him who can eat or who can have enjoyment?" (2:25). The Teacher is saying, "You can't manufacture joy on your own. Joy is a gift. And gifts come from God."

WHAT THIS MEANS FOR YOU

You're probably not a king with unlimited money. But you're running the same experiment the Teacher ran—just with different stuff.

Maybe you think good grades will make you happy. Maybe you think being popular will finally make you feel okay. Maybe you think getting the thing you want—the phone, the followers, the friend group—will fill that weird emptiness inside you.

The Teacher's message isn't "stop wanting things" or "never have fun." His message is, "Don't expect those things to do what only God can do."

Achievements are great. But they fade. Fun is great. But it doesn't last. Wisdom is great. But it can't fix everything. Only God can give you the kind of joy that doesn't disappear when the party ends or the trophy gets dusty.

THE SECRET THE TEACHER DISCOVERED

Here's the big idea: **Meaning isn't something you earn. It's something you receive.** The Teacher tried to build a meaningful life. He tried to achieve his way to happiness. He tried to figure out the secret to satisfaction. And none of it worked—because you can't manufacture meaning on your own.

But when he stopped striving and started receiving? When he saw every meal, every good day, every moment of rest as a gift from God? Everything changed.

Life is still short. Work is still hard. The world is still broken. But joy is possible—not because you earned it, but because God gives it.

The king who had everything finally discovered what mattered most: not what he could build, but what he could receive. And that's available to everyone—even if you don't have a palace or a private jet.

SO WHAT NOW?

Next time you catch yourself thinking, "If I could just get that thing, I'd be happy," remember the Teacher. He got the thing. He got *every*thing. And it wasn't enough. But when he learned to receive life as a gift instead of a trophy to earn? That's when he found what he was looking for.

Eat your food with gratitude.

Do your work with faithfulness.

Enjoy the small moments.

And stop expecting stuff to do what only God can do.

The treadmill will keep running. But you don't have to stay on it forever. Step off. Look up. Receive.

That's where joy lives.

3

A TIME FOR EVERYTHING

Hospitals are weird places if you think about it.

On one floor, a mom is having a baby. There's crying and laughing and people taking pictures. Everyone's excited because a brand-new life just started. At the same time, a few floors up, a family is gathered around a bed saying good-bye to someone they love. It's quiet. People are holding hands. A life is ending.

Birth and death. Joy and grief. Beginnings and endings. All happening in the same building, under the same roof, sometimes in the very same hour.

That's kind of what life is like, isn't it? The happy stuff and the hard stuff don't take turns politely. They bump into each other in the hallway. You can be laughing one minute and crying the next. You can feel grateful and sad at the same time.

Ecclesiastes 3 is about exactly this. It's one of the most famous chapters in the whole Bible—and it's basically saying, "Life doesn't move in straight lines. It moves in seasons. And you don't get to pick which season you're in."

THE TIME POEM

The chapter starts with a poem you've probably heard before, even if you didn't know it came from the Bible: "For everything there is a season, and a time for every matter under heaven." (3:1) Then the Teacher lists a bunch of opposites:

- A time to be born, and a time to die.
- A time to plant, and a time to pull up what's planted.
- A time to cry, and a time to laugh.
- A time to mourn, and a time to dance.
- A time to be quiet, and a time to speak.
- A time for war, and a time for peace.

There are fourteen pairs in total—twenty-eight different "times." And here's what's important: The Teacher isn't giving you advice. He's not saying, "Here's how to know when to laugh and when to cry." He's just describing reality.

Life has all of these things in it. Happy seasons and hard seasons. Seasons when you're building something new and seasons when stuff falls apart. Seasons of friendship and seasons of loneliness. Seasons of winning and seasons of losing.

And you don't get to pick.

YOU'RE NOT IN CONTROL

That's the hard part, isn't it? We like to feel like we're in charge. We make plans. We set goals. We try to control what happens to us. But life doesn't really work that way.

You don't get to decide when someone you love gets sick. You don't get to choose when your family moves to a new city.

You don't get to schedule heartbreak or guarantee that tomorrow will be a good day. The Teacher is saying, "That's okay. That's how it's supposed to be."

The seasons of life aren't random—they're ordered by God. He's the one who sets the times. And even though we can't see the big picture, we can trust that he's holding it all together.

Think of it like being on a road trip but not being the driver. You don't know exactly where you're going or when you'll get there. But if you trust the person behind the wheel, you can relax and enjoy the ride—even when it takes a detour.

ETERNITY IN OUR HEARTS

Here's one of the most beautiful—and confusing—verses in the chapter: "He has made everything beautiful in its time. Also, he has put eternity into man's heart, yet so that he cannot find out what God has done from the beginning to the end" (3:11).

Let's break that down.

First: God makes everything beautiful in its time. That doesn't mean every moment feels good. It means every moment has a place in God's bigger plan. Even the hard seasons have purpose—even if we can't see it yet.

Second: God has put eternity in our hearts. This is huge. Deep down, you know there's more to life than just what you can see. You feel it. You want things to matter. You want your life to mean something. You want to understand how the whole story fits together.

But—and here's the tension—we can't see the whole story. We only get pieces. We see our little slice of time, but we don't get to zoom out and see what God sees.

So we have this big longing inside us—a hunger for meaning, for eternity, for the big picture—but we don't have the ability to satisfy it on our own.

That's frustrating, right? But it's also kind of freeing. Because it means we're not *supposed* to have all the answers. We're supposed to trust the One who does.

SO WHAT DO WE DO?

If we can't control the seasons, and we can't see the whole picture, what are we supposed to do? The Teacher's answer might surprise you: "I perceived that there is nothing better for them than to be joyful and to do good as long as they live; also that everyone should eat and drink and take pleasure in all his toil—this is God's gift to man" (3:12–13).

Wait—that's it? Just... enjoy life?

Yep. That's the wisdom. Not in a "do whatever feels good" kind of way, but in a "receive every day as a gift" kind of way.

You can't control the future. You can't guarantee tomorrow will be easy. But you *can* enjoy today. You can eat a good meal with your family. You can laugh with your friends. You can do your work with a good attitude. You can notice the small good things instead of obsessing over the stuff you can't change.

Joy isn't something you earn. It's something you receive. And it comes from recognizing that even the ordinary moments—lunch with a friend, a sunny afternoon, a project you're proud of—are gifts from God.

WHAT ABOUT WHEN THINGS ARE UNFAIR?

The Teacher doesn't pretend life is always fair. In fact, he admits that sometimes the places that are supposed to be about justice are full of corruption: "In the place of justice, even there was wickedness, and in the place of righteousness, even there was wickedness" (3:16).

That's a real observation. Sometimes the people in charge don't do the right thing. Sometimes bad guys win. Sometimes life feels really, really unfair.

But the Teacher doesn't stop there. He adds: "God will judge the righteous and the wicked, for there is a time for every matter and for every work" (3:17).

In other words: justice might be delayed, but it's not canceled. God sees everything. And just like there's a time for planting and a time for harvesting, there's a time for judgment too. The people who do wrong won't get away with it forever. God has a "time" for that as well.

This doesn't mean we sit back and let bad stuff happen. It means we don't have to carry the weight of fixing everything ourselves. We do what we can, and we trust God with the rest.

DUST AND BREATH

Toward the end of the chapter, the Teacher gets a little intense. He points out that humans and animals both die. We both breathe, and eventually, we both stop breathing. Our bodies go back to the dust.

Why bring that up? Because it keeps us humble.

Sometimes we act like we're invincible. Like we've got everything figured out. Like we're in charge of the universe. But we're not. We're fragile. We're temporary. And that's supposed to make us lean on God instead of ourselves.

The Teacher asks a question: "Who knows whether the human spirit goes upward and the spirit of the animal goes down into the earth?" (3:21).

He's not saying there's no difference between humans and animals—he's saying we can't fully understand what happens after death. But he's also hinting that there *is* something different about us. We're made in God's image. We have eternity in our hearts. And even though we can't see the whole picture, we have reason to hope that death isn't the end of the story.

THE BOTTOM LINE

So what's the takeaway from Ecclesiastes 3?

You're not in control of the seasons—but God is. There will be happy times and hard times. Times to laugh and times to cry. Times when everything's going great and times when nothing makes sense. You don't get to pick. But you can trust the One who does.

You won't understand everything—and that's okay. God has put eternity in your heart, which means you'll always want more than this world can give. But instead of driving yourself crazy trying to figure it all out, you can rest in the fact that God sees the whole story even when you don't.

Joy is the right response. Not fake happiness. Not pretending everything is fine. But real, grateful, ordinary joy—receiving each day as a gift, noticing the good stuff, and trusting God with the hard stuff.

Life is like that hospital—birth and death, laughter and tears, all happening under the same roof. The seasons come whether we're ready or not. But the God who made the seasons

is also the God who walks through them with you.
And that makes all the difference.

33

4

YOU WEREN'T MEANT TO DO THIS ALONE

Have you ever felt completely alone—even in a room full of people? Maybe you were going through something hard, and everyone around you just kept living their normal lives like nothing was happening. They were laughing, posting pictures, talking about stuff that didn't matter. And you were carrying something so heavy you could barely breathe.

That's one of the loneliest feelings in the world. It's not just the pain that hurts—it's the feeling that nobody sees it.

Ecclesiastes 4 is about that kind of loneliness. But it's also about something else: how we're not designed to go through life by ourselves. The Teacher looks around at the world—at all its unfairness, competition, and exhaustion—and points to one thing that makes the hard stuff bearable.

Relationships.

WHEN LIFE IS UNFAIR

The chapter starts with something heavy. The Teacher looks at the world and sees people being crushed by other people. The powerful taking advantage of the weak. The rich stepping on the poor. The bullies winning and the victims crying with no one to help.

"I saw the tears of the oppressed—and they have no comforter" (4:1). The phrase "no comforter" shows up twice in the verse, like the Teacher is making sure we don't miss it. The worst part of suffering isn't always the suffering itself. It's suffering *alone*. It's crying and feeling like nobody sees.

The Teacher doesn't try to explain why bad things happen. He doesn't give a neat little answer. He just names it. He says: "Yeah, this is real. This is awful. And I see it."

Sometimes that's where wisdom starts—not with answers, but with honesty. Before you can fix a problem, you have to admit it exists.

And here's the important part: Even when nobody on earth sees your tears, God does. The Teacher will get there eventually. But for now, he wants us to feel the weight of what it's like when comfort is missing.

THE COMPARISON TRAP

After talking about unfairness, the Teacher zooms in on something sneakier: jealousy. "I saw that all toil and all skill in work come from a man's envy of his neighbor" (4:4). In other words, a lot of the time, we're not working hard because we love what we're doing. We're working hard because we're comparing ourselves to someone else.

Think about it. You study harder because someone else got a better grade. You practice more because someone else made the team. You want nicer stuff because someone else already has it. You post something online hoping to get more likes than someone else.

That's envy. And it's exhausting.

The problem with envy is that it never lets you rest. Even when you win, you're already looking at the next person to beat. Even when you get what you wanted, you're already noticing what someone else has. It's like running on a treadmill that never stops—lots of effort, but you never actually get anywhere.

The Teacher calls this "chasing after the wind." You can't catch the wind. And you can't catch satisfaction when jealousy is doing the driving.

THE LAZY TRAP

But here's the thing: The Teacher isn't saying you should just give up and do nothing. He actually has a warning for lazy people too: "The fool folds his hands and ruins himself" (4:5). Basically, if you don't do *anything*, that's also a disaster. Laziness destroys you from the inside out.

So envy pushes you too hard, and laziness doesn't push you at all. Where's the balance?

Here it is: "Better is a handful of quietness than two hands full of toil and a striving after wind" (4:6). Picture someone frantically grabbing as much stuff as they can with both hands. They're stressed, sweaty, anxious—always reaching for more.

Now picture someone calmly holding just what they need with one hand. They've got enough. They're at peace.

The Teacher is saying that contentment beats competition. Having less with peace is better than having more with stress. You don't have to be the best at everything. You don't have to beat everyone around you. Sometimes "enough" really is enough.

THE LONELY WORKAHOLIC

Next, the Teacher paints a picture that might sound familiar—even if you're young.

Imagine someone who works all the time. They're always busy, always productive, always chasing the next thing. They've got money and success and a full schedule. But they have no one to share it with. No close friends. No real connection. Just... stuff. "There was a man all alone; he had neither son nor brother. There was no end to his toil, yet his eyes were not content with his wealth. 'For whom am I toiling,' he asked, 'and why am I depriving myself of enjoyment?'" (4:8).

That question is haunting: "Who am I doing all this for?"

If you can't answer that question—if there's no one in your life you're working *with* or working *for*—then something's gone wrong. Success without relationships is hollow. Achievements don't mean much if you've got no one to celebrate them with. The Teacher calls this "a miserable business." And he's right.

TWO ARE BETTER THAN ONE

Now comes the good part. After all that heaviness, the Teacher gives us something hopeful: "Two are better than one, because they have a good reward for their toil" (4:9). This isn't complicated. Life is better with people. Work is better with partners. Hardships are better with friends. That's the design. The Teacher gives three examples:

1. When you fall, someone picks you up. "If they fall, one will lift up his fellow. But woe to him who is alone when he falls and has not another to lift him up!" (4:10). Everyone falls sometimes. Everyone messes up, gets hurt, hits rock bottom. The difference between making it and not making it often comes down to one thing: Is someone there to help you back up?

2. When it's cold, someone keeps you warm. "If two lie together, they keep warm, but how can one keep warm alone?" (4:11). Back in ancient times, people traveling at night could freeze if they were alone. Staying close to someone else kept them alive. Life can feel cold too—not physically, but emotionally. When hard times come, relationships are like warmth. They don't fix everything, but they keep you going.

3. When you're attacked, someone has your back. "Though one may be overpowered, two can defend themselves" (4:12). Life throws punches. Temptations come. Discouragement hits. If you're all by yourself, it's easy to get knocked down. But if someone's standing beside you? You've got a fighting chance.

Then comes the famous line: "A cord of three strands is not quickly broken" (4:12). One rope is easy to snap. Two ropes twisted together? Stronger. Three? Nearly impossible to break. That's what real friendship looks like. That's what real community does. It multiplies your strength.

THE RISE AND FALL OF FAME

The chapter ends with a weird little story about kings and fame—and honestly, it's kind of depressing.

The Teacher describes a young guy who rises from nothing to become super popular. Everyone loves him. He goes from prison to the palace. The crowds cheer. It looks like he's got it made.

But then? "Those who come later will not be pleased with him" (4:16). The next generation forgets him. New heroes take his place. The applause fades. The fame disappears.

Sound familiar? Think about how fast celebrities rise and fall today. Someone can be everywhere one year and totally forgotten the next. Popularity is like smoke—it looks solid, but it vanishes when you try to hold onto it.

The Teacher's point? Don't build your life on applause. Crowds are fickle. Trends change. What people love today, they'll ignore tomorrow. Fame can't give you what relationships can. Popularity can't replace real connection.

WHAT THIS CHAPTER TEACHES US

Ecclesiastes 4 shows us a bunch of ways life can go wrong:

> **Oppression**—when powerful people hurt weaker ones.
> **Envy**—when comparison drives you crazy.
> **Laziness**—when you give up and do nothing.
> **Isolation**—when you succeed but have no one to share it with.
> **Fame**—when popularity becomes your identity.

But underneath all of that is one big truth: **You weren't made to do life alone.** God designed us for relationships. For community. For people who pick us up when we fall, keep us warm when life gets cold, and stand with us when things get hard.

That doesn't mean relationships are easy. They're not. People let you down. Friendships are messy. Community takes effort.

But the alternative—going through life solo, chasing success nobody celebrates, carrying pain nobody sees—is way worse.

SO WHAT DO YOU DO?

Here's the practical stuff:

Stop comparing. You don't have to beat everyone else. You just have to be faithful with what you've got. Contentment beats competition every time.

Find your people. Not a hundred followers online—real people. A few friends who actually know you. A community where you can be honest. People who will lift you up when you fall.

Be that person for someone else. Don't just look for comfort—be a comforter. If the biggest tragedy is suffering alone, then one of the most important things you can do is make sure the people around you aren't alone either.

Remember that God sees. Even when no one else does. Even when you're crying and it feels like nobody cares. God sees. God remembers. And God walks through the hard seasons with you.

Ecclesiastes 4 is honest about how hard life can be. But it's also hopeful—because it shows us the way through. Two are better than one. A cord of three strands isn't easily broken. You weren't meant to chase the wind alone.

So don't.

5

WATCH YOUR MOUTH (ESPECIALLY AROUND GOD)

Have you ever walked into a room and instantly known you needed to be quiet? Maybe it was a courtroom on a school field trip. The moment the judge walked in, everyone stood up. Nobody was joking around anymore. Nobody was looking at their phone. Something about the room just demanded respect.

Or maybe you've been at a hospital visiting someone really sick. You didn't talk loud. You didn't ramble about random stuff. You whispered. You said what mattered and left out what didn't. The moment felt too serious for small talk.

There are places in life where your words shrink—not because you're scared, but because you recognize something bigger than yourself is happening. Ecclesiastes 5 is about bringing that same attitude to God.

GUARD YOUR STEPS

The chapter opens with a warning you don't hear very often: "Guard your steps when you go to the house of God" (5:1). Back in the Teacher's day, "the house of God" meant the temple—the place where people went to worship, pray, and make sacrifices. It was supposed to be a holy place where heaven and earth met.

But apparently, a lot of people were treating it like... no big deal. They'd stroll in casually, say a bunch of stuff, make a bunch of promises, and leave without really thinking about what they were doing.

The Teacher says: Don't be that person. When you come to God, slow down. Pay attention. This isn't like walking into a fast-food restaurant where you rattle off your order and move on. This is approaching the Creator of the universe. The One who spoke the stars into existence. The One who knows every thought in your head before you think it.

That deserves some respect.

LISTEN MORE, TALK LESS

Here's the main point of this section: "Draw near to listen rather than to offer the sacrifice of fools" (5:1). In other words: when you come to God, listen first. Don't just start talking.

The "sacrifice of fools" doesn't mean they brought the wrong animal to the temple. It means they brought the wrong heart. They were going through the motions—showing up, doing religious stuff—but they weren't actually paying attention. They weren't humble. They weren't ready to hear from God. They were just performing.

The Teacher is saying: God isn't impressed by noise. He's not impressed by how many words you say or how spiritual you sound. What he wants is for you to actually *listen*.

Think about the people in your life who talk all the time.

You know the type—they never stop to hear what anyone else is saying. They're just waiting for their turn to talk again. That's annoying with people. It's even worse with God.

The wise person comes to God and says, "I'm here to listen. I'm here to receive. What do you want to say to me?" The fool comes to God and says, "Here's my list of demands. Here's what I need. Here's what I think you should do."

Big difference.

GOD IS IN HEAVEN. YOU ARE ON EARTH.

The Teacher gives a reason for all of this: "God is in heaven and you are on earth, so let your words be few" (5:2). That's not meant to make you feel small in a bad way. It's meant to remind you of reality. God isn't your buddy who you can casually chat with about whatever. He's the eternal, all-powerful, all-knowing Creator of everything.

Does that mean you can't talk to him? No way. The Bible is full of people talking to God—sometimes even arguing with him. But even those conversations happened with respect. They happened with an awareness that God is God and we're not.

When you really understand that, your words naturally shrink. Not because you're scared, but because you realize you don't need to say a lot. God already knows what you need. He already knows what's in your heart. You don't have to impress him with long prayers or fancy words.

Just be honest. And be brief.

THE DANGER OF MAKING PROMISES

Now the Teacher shifts to something really practical: making promises to God. "When you make a vow to God, do not delay in fulfilling it. He has no pleasure in fools; fulfill your vow. It is better not to make a vow than to make one and not fulfill it" (5:4–5).

You've probably done this. Everyone has. You're in a tough spot. Maybe you're scared, or stressed, or desperate. And you pray something like: "God, if you get me out of this, I'll read my Bible every day. I'll be nicer to my sibling. I'll never complain again. I'll do *anything*."

And in that moment, you totally mean it.

But then the crisis passes. The stress goes away. And suddenly that promise you made? It feels way harder to keep. So you just... forget about it. You move on. You hope God didn't take you too seriously.

The Teacher says: He did.

God takes your words seriously—even the ones you said when you were panicking. If you make a promise to God, he expects you to keep it. And if you can't keep it, he'd rather you just not make it in the first place.

That's a hard thing to hear, but it's important. It means we should be careful about what we say to God. Not because he's trying to trap us, but because words matter. Promises matter. Integrity matters. Don't make promises in the heat of the moment that you have no intention of keeping. And if you do make a promise, follow through.

DON'T MAKE EXCUSES

The Teacher imagines someone who makes a vow and then later tries to weasel out of it: "Do not let your mouth lead you into sin. And do not protest to the temple messenger, 'My vow was a mistake'" (5:6). In other words: don't make a promise to God and then show up later saying, "Oh, I didn't really mean that. It was just something I said in the moment. Can we forget about it?"

That's not how it works. God isn't fooled by excuses. He knows what you said. He knows what you meant. And he expects you to stand by your word.

This might sound intense, but the Teacher isn't trying to scare you—he's trying to protect you. Because when you get in the habit of saying things you don't mean, you start losing your integrity. You become someone whose words can't be trusted. And that affects everything—your relationship with God, your relationships with people, even your relationship with yourself.

The solution? Don't say things you don't mean. Be slow to speak. Think before you promise.

DREAMS AND WORDS

Here's a weird little verse: "For when dreams increase and words grow many, there is vanity" (5:7). What does that mean?

Think about when you're stressed or overwhelmed. You might have crazy, chaotic dreams at night—your brain just running wild because you've got too much going on. The Teacher says that's what happens to your words when your heart is all over the place. You just start talking and talking without really thinking.

Lots of dreams = an overwhelmed mind.

Lots of words = an overwhelmed heart.

And both of them lead to emptiness. To vapor. To nothing solid.

The point is this: When your insides are chaotic, your outsides get chaotic too. You say things you don't mean. You make promises you can't keep. You perform instead of actually connecting with God.

The cure? Slow down. Get quiet. Let your heart settle before your mouth starts moving.

FEAR GOD

The Teacher ends this section with a single, powerful phrase: "But God is the one you must fear" (5:7). That word "fear" can be confusing. It doesn't mean "be terrified of God" like he's some scary monster waiting to punish you. It means reverence. Respect. Awe.

It means recognizing that God is bigger than you, wiser than you, and more powerful than you—and that's a good thing. It means approaching him with humility instead of arrogance. It means letting your words be shaped by who he is, not just by what you want.

The fear of God is the antidote to almost everything the Teacher has talked about in Ecclesiastes:

- Oppression? People who fear God can't treat others like garbage.
- Envy? People who fear God don't need to compete with everyone.
- Loneliness? People who fear God learn humility and real connection.
- Empty religion? People who fear God actually mean what they say.

The fear of God isn't about being scared. It's about being grounded. It's about knowing the truth: God is God, and you're not. And when you live from that truth, everything else starts to make sense.

WHAT THIS MEANS FOR YOU

Okay, so what does this look like practically?

When you pray, slow down. Don't just rattle off a list of things you want. Take a breath. Remember who you're talking to. And spend some time just listening.

Be careful what you promise. Whether it's to God or to other people, don't say things you don't mean. Your words matter. Make them count.

Don't treat God like a vending machine. You can't just put in a prayer and expect to get what you want. Worship isn't a transaction—it's a relationship. And relationships require respect.

Let your words be few. Not because God doesn't want to hear from you, but because fewer honest words are better than a flood of empty ones.

Fear God. Not with terror, but with reverence. Let your whole life be shaped by the reality that God is real, he's watching, and he cares about how you live.

THE POINT OF IT ALL

Ecclesiastes 5 isn't saying, "Never talk to God." It's saying, "Be careful how you talk to God." He's not impressed by performance. He doesn't need your religious show. He's not moved by long prayers or dramatic promises. What he wants is honesty. Humility. Reverence. A heart that listens before it speaks.

In a world full of noise, God is waiting for people who will be quiet. In a world full of empty promises, God is looking for people who keep their word. In a world full of vapor, God alone is solid.

So guard your steps. Let your words be few. And fear the God who is in heaven—because he's the only one worth fearing.

6

WHEN HAVING EVERYTHING ISN'T ENOUGH

You know that feeling when you sit down to watch something, open Netflix or Disney+ or whatever you use, and you just... scroll? There are literally thousands of options. Movies you've been meaning to watch. Shows everyone's talking about. And after fifteen minutes of scrolling, you say the thing every modern human has said: "There's nothing to watch."

It makes no sense. You have more options than any generation in history. More entertainment at your fingertips than kings and queens could have dreamed of a hundred years ago. And somehow... you're bored.

That weird frustration—having tons of stuff but still feeling empty—is exactly what Ecclesiastes 5–6 are about.

THE MAN WHO HAD EVERYTHING

The Teacher tells a story about a guy who seems to have it all. Wealth. Possessions. Respect. Basically everything the ancient world said you needed to be happy. But here's the twist: "God does not give him the ability to enjoy them" (6:2).

Wait—what? He has everything but can't enjoy any of it? Yep. And the Teacher says this is one of the saddest things he's ever seen.

Imagine a huge, beautiful house. Fancy furniture. A long dining table with enough seats for a big family. But every night, the guy who owns it eats alone. No laughter. No conversation. No warmth. Just him, sitting in the dark, surrounded by stuff that doesn't make him happy.

That's the picture the Teacher paints. A man with a full house and an empty heart. A guy who spent his whole life collecting things but never actually enjoyed them.

And the worst part? When he dies, someone else gets all his stuff—and *they* enjoy it. He did all the work. Someone else gets the reward.

WHY MORE STUFF DOESN'T EQUAL MORE HAPPINESS

Here's what the Teacher figured out: "Whoever loves money never has enough; whoever loves wealth is never satisfied with their income" (5:10).

Think about it. Have you ever wanted something really badly—a game, a phone, a pair of shoes—and thought, "If I just get this, I'll be happy"?

And then you got it. And it was cool... for like a week. Maybe a month. But eventually, you started wanting the *next* thing. The upgrade. The newer version. Something better.

That's what the Teacher is talking about. Money and stuff don't satisfy you—they just make you want more money and more stuff. Your appetite grows faster than your bank account ever could. It's like trying to fill a bucket with a hole in the bottom. You keep pouring, but it never fills up.

THE RICH GUY WHO CAN'T SLEEP

Here's a line that might surprise you: "The sleep of a laborer is sweet, whether they eat little or much, but as for the rich, their abundance permits them no sleep" (5:12).

The person who works hard and doesn't have much? They sleep great. They're tired from honest work, and their minds aren't cluttered with a million worries.

But the rich guy? He's up all night. Stressing about his investments. Worrying about losing what he has. Anxious about people trying to take his stuff. His wealth doesn't give him peace—it steals it.

The Teacher isn't saying being poor is automatically better than being rich. He's saying contentment is better than anxiety. And sometimes, the more you have, the more anxious you become.

It's possible to have a simple life and sleep like a baby. And it's possible to have a mansion and lie awake staring at the ceiling every night.

YOU CAN'T TAKE IT WITH YOU

The Teacher drops a truth bomb that everyone knows but nobody likes to think about: "Everyone comes naked from their mother's womb, and as everyone comes, so they depart. They take nothing from their toil that they can carry in their hands" (5:15). You came into the world with nothing. And when you leave, you're taking nothing with you.

No matter how much money you make, how many trophies

you win, how much stuff you collect—none of it goes with you when you die. It all stays here. Someone else gets it.

That's not meant to be depressing. It's meant to be freeing. Because if you can't take it with you anyway, why spend your whole life stressing about it? The Teacher calls it "chasing the wind." You're running after something you can never actually hold.

WHEN WEALTH BECOMES A CURSE

Here's where it gets really intense. The Teacher describes a man who hoards everything he has. He doesn't share. He doesn't enjoy. He just... accumulates. And then something bad happens—he loses it all. "Riches hoarded to the harm of their owners" (5:13).

His money didn't help him. It hurt him. He spent his whole life obsessing over wealth, and in the end, it destroyed him.

The Teacher says this guy "eats in darkness, with great frustration, affliction and anger" (5:17). That's the emotional life of someone whose heart is consumed by greed. Lonely. Bitter. Angry. Even though his bank account is full, his soul is starving.

A STILLBORN CHILD?

Okay, this is a weird one, but stick with me. The Teacher says something shocking: "A stillborn child is better off than him" (6:3). He's talking about the guy who has everything—wealth, kids, long life—but can't enjoy any of it. The Teacher says a baby who never even gets to live is better off than that guy.

Why? Because the baby never experiences the long, slow misery of a joyless life. The man lives for decades, surrounded by blessings, but never tastes a single one.

The Teacher isn't saying stillbirth is good. He's saying living without joy is that bad. It's one of the saddest conditions a human being can be in: having everything and enjoying nothing.

SO WHAT'S THE SOLUTION?

Right when things seem totally hopeless, the Teacher offers a different way: "This is what I have observed to be good: that it is appropriate for a person to eat, to drink and to find satisfaction in their toilsome labor under the sun during the few days of life God has given them—for this is their lot" (5:18). Translation: Enjoy what you have. Receive each day as a gift. Don't obsess over more—appreciate what's already in front of you.

This isn't about being lazy or settling for less. It's about contentment. It's about recognizing that every meal, every good day, every moment of rest is a gift from God.

And here's the key line: "When God gives someone wealth and possessions, and the ability to enjoy them... this is a gift of God" (5:19). Catch that? The ability to enjoy what you have is itself a gift. Some people have tons of stuff and can't enjoy any of it. Other people have very little and are genuinely happy. The difference isn't the stuff—it's whether God has given them the ability to receive it with gratitude.

APPETITE VS. EYES

Near the end of this section, the Teacher says something simple but profound: "Better what the eye sees than the roving of the appetite" (6:9). Your "appetite" is that restless craving for more—more stuff, more experiences, more everything. It's never satisfied. It always wants the next thing. Your "eyes" are what's right in front of you. What you already have. What's actually here, today.

The Teacher says: Stop chasing what you don't have. Start enjoying what you do. That's contentment. That's wisdom. That's peace.

NOBODY KNOWS THE FUTURE

The section ends with some honest questions: "Who knows what is good for a person in life, during the few and meaningless days they pass through like a shadow? Who can tell them what will happen under the sun after they are gone?" (6:12).

The answer is: nobody. You don't know what tomorrow holds. You don't know what's going to happen after you're gone. You can't control the future. So why waste your life stressing about it?

The Teacher isn't being depressing. He's being liberating. If you can't control the future, stop obsessing over it. If you can't take your stuff with you, stop hoarding it. If more money won't make you happy, stop chasing it like it will. Instead, receive today as a gift. Enjoy what God has put in front of you. Trust him with the rest.

WHAT THIS MEANS FOR YOU

You might not be rich. You probably don't have a mansion or a stock portfolio. But the same temptation hits everyone—the belief that more will make you happy. More followers. More popularity. More stuff. More success.

The Teacher says it won't. More won't fill the hole. More won't quiet the restlessness. More won't give you peace. Only

God can do that. And he does it not by giving you everything you want, but by giving you the ability to enjoy what you already have.

So here's the challenge:

Stop scrolling. Whether it's streaming apps, social media, or your own ambitions—stop constantly searching for the next thing.

Look around. What do you already have that's good? A family who loves you? Food on the table? A warm bed? Friends? Those aren't small things. Those are gifts.

Say thank you. Gratitude is the antidote to greed. When you start thanking God for what you have, you stop obsessing over what you don't.

Receive today. You don't know what tomorrow holds. But you've got today. That's enough.

THE BOTTOM LINE

Ecclesiastes 5–6 is about one big idea: **Having everything doesn't help if you can't enjoy it.** Joy isn't something you earn by collecting enough stuff. Joy is a gift from God—and it comes to people who receive life with open hands instead of clenched fists.

The man in the big, lonely house spent his life accumulating and never enjoying. Don't be that guy.

The person with a simple life and a grateful heart sleeps well and lives well. Be that person.

You weren't made to chase the wind forever.

You were made to receive the gift.

So stop scrolling. Look up. And enjoy what's already there.

7

THE WISDOM YOU DIDN'T KNOW YOU NEEDED

You probably have a drawer somewhere in your house full of random stuff. Maybe there's a flashlight your parents bought "just in case." A first-aid kit nobody's opened in years. Batteries. Tape. Instruction manuals for things you forgot you had.

Most of that stuff seems pointless—until suddenly it isn't. The power goes out, and you need the flashlight. You cut your finger, and you need a bandage. Something breaks, and the manual actually helps.

Wisdom works the same way.

There are certain truths you don't think you need—until life puts you in a situation where you desperately do. And here's the uncomfortable part: Some of the most important wisdom comes from experiences you would *never* choose.

Ecclesiastes 7 is full of that kind of wisdom. It's not the easy, feel-good stuff. It's the truths that come from hard experiences—funerals, correction, disappointment, waiting. The Teacher isn't being negative. He's being honest about where real growth happens.

And spoiler alert: It's usually not at the party.

WHY FUNERALS TEACH MORE THAN BIRTHDAYS

The chapter opens with a statement that might make you uncomfortable: "It is better to go to a house of mourning than to go to a house of feasting" (7:2).

Wait—a funeral is better than a party? Really?

The Teacher isn't saying parties are bad. He's saying funerals teach you things parties can't.

Think about it. At a party, everyone's laughing, eating, taking selfies, having fun. Nothing wrong with that. But it's easy to float through a party without thinking about anything deep.

A funeral is different. When someone dies, you can't avoid the big questions. You think about what really matters. You realize life is short. You pay attention to the people you love. You stop caring about dumb stuff.

The Teacher says, "The living should take this to heart" (7:2). In other words, let the reality of death shape the way you live. Not in a morbid, depressing way—but in a way that helps you focus on what actually counts.

Most people run from hard stuff. They fill their lives with noise and entertainment and distraction. But the wise person is willing to sit in the hard moments, because that's where the deepest lessons live.

SORROW CAN MAKE YOU BETTER

Here's another surprising line: "Sorrow is better than laughter, for by sadness of face the heart is made glad" (7:3).

Okay, that sounds weird. How can sadness make your heart glad?

The Teacher isn't saying you should try to be sad all the

time. He's saying that sorrow—when you actually face it—can do something good in you.

Think about a time when something hard happened. Maybe you lost someone. Maybe a friendship fell apart. Maybe you failed at something important. In that moment, it hurt. But looking back, did it change you?

Hard experiences have a way of carving out space in your heart. They make you more compassionate. They help you appreciate good things you used to take for granted. They teach you what matters. Laughter is great. But laughter doesn't usually change you. Sorrow can.

That's why the Teacher says, "The heart of the wise is in the house of mourning, but the heart of fools is in the house of mirth" (7:4). The wise person doesn't run from hard stuff. They know that depth comes from facing reality, not escaping it.

WHY CRITICISM BEATS FLATTERY

Next, the Teacher gives you a truth you probably don't want to hear: "It is better to heed the rebuke of a wise person than to listen to the song of fools" (7:5). A "rebuke" is when someone tells you something you're doing wrong. It doesn't feel good. Nobody wakes up thinking, "I hope someone corrects me today!"

But the Teacher says it's better than the "song of fools"—which is basically flattery, empty compliments, people telling you what you want to hear. Why? Because correction helps you grow. Flattery keeps you stuck.

Imagine you're terrible at something—let's say basketball. You brick every shot, trip over your own feet, and can barely dribble. Now imagine you have two friends:

- Friend A says, "You're amazing! Best player I've ever seen!"
- Friend B says, "Hey, your form is off. Let me show you how to fix it."

Who's actually helping you? Friend B. Even though it stings a little to hear.

The Teacher compares the laughter of fools to "the crackling of thorns under a pot" (7:6). Thorns catch fire fast, crackle loudly, and burn out in seconds. They make a lot of noise but produce no real heat. That's what foolish flattery is like. It sounds nice for a second, but it doesn't warm you or help you grow.

PATIENCE BEATS PRIDE

Here's a line worth memorizing: "The end of a matter is better than its beginning, and patience is better than pride" (7:8). Beginnings are exciting. New projects, new goals, new relationships—they're full of hope and energy. But beginnings don't tell you much. It's the *end* that shows what something really was.

Think about a race. The start is fun—everyone's pumped, the gun goes off, you're sprinting. But what matters is how you finish. Did you keep going when it got hard? Did you pace yourself? Did you cross the finish line?

The Teacher says patience is better than pride. Pride says, "I want results now. I deserve success immediately. Why is this taking so long?" Pride is impatient, demanding, and easily frustrated. Patience says, "I'll keep going. I'll trust the process. I don't control the timing, but I'll stay faithful."

Patience is humble. Pride is not.

And here's a related warning: "Do not be quickly provoked in your spirit, for anger resides in the lap of fools" (7:9). Anger often comes from impatience. When things don't go your way, when people disappoint you, when life doesn't match your expectations—it's easy to get mad.

But the Teacher says anger "resides" in fools. It moves in and stays. Wise people don't let anger become a permanent guest in their hearts.

STOP SAYING THE OLD DAYS WERE BETTER

Here's one that might hit close to home: "Do not say, 'Why were the old days better than these?' For it is not wise to ask such questions" (7:10). Ever heard an adult say something like, "Back in my day, things were so much better"? Maybe your grandparents talk about how great life was when they were young. Maybe you even catch yourself thinking, "Last year was so much better than this year." The Teacher says: Stop it.

Nostalgia—that feeling that the past was better—is usually a lie. The past wasn't actually better. You're just remembering the good parts and forgetting the hard stuff.

Every generation has problems. Every era has challenges. Wishing you were back in some "golden age" keeps you from living faithfully now. Wisdom doesn't waste time longing for yesterday. It receives today.

WISDOM IS VALUABLE—BUT LIMITED

The Teacher says something really important near the end of this section: "Wisdom, like an inheritance, is a good thing and benefits those who see the sun" (7:11). Wisdom is good. It protects you, guides you, helps you make better decisions. It's like shade on a hot day—it shelters you from the worst of life's heat.

But then the Teacher adds this: "Consider what God has done: Who can straighten what he has made crooked?" (7:13). Even wisdom has limits. You can't control everything. You can't fix everything. Some things in life are just... bent. Broken. Complicated. And no amount of cleverness can straighten them out. That's not depressing—it's freeing. Because it means you're not supposed to have all the answers. You're not supposed to control the future. You're just supposed to trust the God who does.

The Teacher puts it like this: "When times are good, be happy; but when times are bad, consider this: God has made the one as well as the other" (7:14). Good days come from God. Hard days come from God too. Not because God is cruel, but because he's shaping you into someone deeper, stronger, and more dependent on him. Your job isn't to figure out why. Your job is to stay faithful in both seasons.

WHAT THIS MEANS FOR YOU

Ecclesiastes 7 is the Teacher's way of slowing you down and sobering you up. It's not pessimistic—it's realistic. And realism is the soil where wisdom grows. Here's what to take away:

Don't run from hard stuff. Funerals, failures, disappointments—they hurt. But they also teach. The wise person doesn't avoid pain. They let it shape them.

Listen to correction. It stings, but it helps. Flattery feels good, but it keeps you stuck. Find people who will tell you the truth—and actually listen to them.

Be patient, not proud. You don't control the timing. You don't control the outcome. But you can control whether you stay faithful. Patience trusts God. Pride demands its own way.

Stop romanticizing the past. Yesterday wasn't better. It was just earlier. Receive today as the gift it is.

Accept your limits. Wisdom is valuable, but it can't straighten everything. Some things only God can fix. Let that humble you—and let it point you back to him.

THE QUIET CENTER

Ecclesiastes 7 isn't flashy. It doesn't promise quick fixes or five easy steps to happiness. It's slower, deeper, and more honest than that. The Teacher wants you to be the kind of person who can walk into any room—whether it's a party or a funeral—and carry the same awareness: Life is short, God is in control, and every season has something to teach you.

That's wisdom. Not the kind that makes you look smart. The kind that makes you actually live well.

So take a breath. Slow down. Let the hard stuff do its work.

And trust that the God who made both the good days and the bad ones knows exactly what he's doing.

8

YOU CAN'T STRAIGHTEN WHAT GOD MADE CROOKED

Have you ever been to a hardware store and watched someone pick out wood? They grab a board, roll it on the ground, hold it up to their eye like they're aiming a bow, flip it over, squint at it again, and finally mutter: "Nope. This one's bent too."

Here's the thing about wood: It's almost never perfectly straight. It has knots and curves and weird spots where the grain twists. You can sand it, clamp it, work with it—but you can't make it forget the tree it came from.

The Teacher says something similar about life: "Consider what God has done: Who can straighten what he has made crooked?" (7:13). In other words, stop shouting at the bent pieces.

Some parts of life just aren't straight. Relationships get messy. Plans fall apart. People get sick when they shouldn't. Good people suffer. Bad people seem to win. You can't force everything into neat, tidy lines—no matter how hard you try.

And that's not because you're doing something wrong. It's because life isn't a factory-made product. It's more like a tree— knotted, twisted, beautiful in its own way, and shaped by forces bigger than us.

GOOD DAYS AND BAD DAYS BOTH COME FROM GOD

The Teacher gives some really practical advice here: "When times are good, be happy; but when times are bad, consider this: God has made the one as well as the other" (7:14).

Most of us treat good days like they're normal and bad days like something went wrong. But the Teacher says both come from God. He's not surprised by either one.

Good days are gifts. Enjoy them! Don't feel guilty about happiness. But also don't expect every day to be like that.

Bad days are teachers. They make you think. They humble you. They remind you that you're not in control.

Here's the tricky part: "So that no one can discover anything about their future" (7:14). God mixes up the good and the bad partly so we can't predict what's coming next. If life were totally predictable, we'd stop depending on God. We'd trust our own plans instead of trusting him.

Not knowing the future isn't a bug—it's a feature. It keeps us humble.

WHY BEING "SUPER RIGHTEOUS" CAN ACTUALLY HURT YOU

Okay, this next part sounds weird at first: "Do not be overrighteous, neither be overwise—why destroy yourself?" (7:16).

Wait—can you be too good? Isn't that the goal?

Here's what the Teacher means: Some people think if they're religious enough, strict enough, perfect enough, then God *has* to bless them. They treat being good like a formula—do the right things, and life will work out.

That's not how it works. And people who think that way

often crash hard when life doesn't cooperate. They get bitter, angry, or burnt out.

Being "overrighteous" doesn't mean being too good. It means being too confident that your goodness gives you control over outcomes. It's a sneaky kind of pride.

Then the Teacher adds: "Do not be overwicked, and do not be a fool—why die before your time?" (7:17). This isn't saying "be a little bit wicked." It's warning against the opposite extreme—the person who sees that life is unfair and thinks, "Well, nothing matters, so I'll just do whatever I want." That's also destructive. Sin has consequences, even if they're not immediate.

So what's the answer? "Whoever fears God will avoid all extremes" (7:18). Fearing God keeps you balanced. You don't become a religious robot who thinks you can earn God's favor. But you also don't give up on doing what's right. You stay humble, trust God, and keep walking.

NOBODY'S PERFECT

Here's a line that might sting a little: "Indeed, there is no one on earth who is righteous, no one who does what is right and never sins" (7:20). Nobody. Not your preacher. Not your parents. Not that kid at school who seems like they've got everything together. Not you.

Everyone messes up. Everyone sins. Everyone falls short.

That's not meant to make you feel hopeless. It's meant to make you *humble*. When you remember that you're not perfect, you stop expecting everyone else to be perfect too.

Speaking of which...

DON'T TAKE EVERYTHING SO PERSONALLY

The Teacher gives some surprisingly practical advice: "Do not pay attention to every word people say, or you may hear your servant cursing you—for you know in your heart that many times you yourself have cursed others" (7:21–22).

Ever hear someone say something about you that stung? Maybe it was a careless comment. Maybe it was gossip. Maybe it was a frustrated remark that wasn't even meant to be serious.

The Teacher says: Don't obsess over it. Not every word someone says deserves your full emotional attention. People vent. People exaggerate. People say dumb stuff when they're tired or frustrated. If you take everything personally, you'll be miserable all the time.

And here's the kicker: You've done the same thing. You've said things about people that weren't fair. You've complained, vented, or said something you didn't totally mean. We all have. So give people the same grace you'd want them to give you. Don't magnify every careless word into a crisis.

WISDOM HAS LIMITS

Now the Teacher gets really honest—almost confessional: "All this I tested by wisdom. I said, 'I am determined to be wise'— but this was beyond me. Whatever exists is far off and most profound—who can discover it?" (7:23–24). He tried. He *really* tried. He studied, examined, tested, and searched for answers. And you know what he found? The deeper he dug, the more mysterious life became.

That's frustrating, right? You'd think that the smarter you get, the more you'd understand. But the Teacher says it's the opposite. Wisdom shows you how much you *don't* know. It reveals the mystery, not the answers.

This isn't meant to make you give up on learning. It's meant to keep you humble. You'll never have it all figured out. And that's okay—because God does.

WHAT WENT WRONG WITH HUMANITY

The chapter ends with a really important statement: "This only have I found: God created mankind upright, but they have gone in search of many schemes" (7:29). That's basically the whole story of the Bible in one sentence.

God made people good. We were designed to be "upright"—straight, aligned with his purposes, living in harmony with him. But then we started scheming. We invented our own plans, chased our own desires, and wandered away from the design.

That's why the world is crooked. Not because God messed up. Because we did. The brokenness you see in the world—the unfairness, the pain, the confusion—isn't God's fault. It's the result of humanity going our own way instead of his.

That's humbling. But it's also hopeful. Because if we broke it, then it's something God can fix. And that's exactly what the rest of the Bible is about.

WHAT THIS MEANS FOR YOU

Ecclesiastes 7:13–29 is one of the most realistic parts of the whole book. The Teacher doesn't sugarcoat anything. He admits:

- Life is crooked, and you can't straighten it.
- Good days and bad days both come from God.

- Being super religious won't guarantee good outcomes.
- Nobody is perfect—including you.
- People say dumb stuff, and so do you.
- Wisdom has limits; you'll never figure it all out.
- Humanity is broken because we chose our own way instead of God's.

That sounds heavy. But here's the good news buried in all of it: You don't have to have it all figured out. You don't have to be perfect. You don't have to control the outcomes. You don't have to straighten every crooked thing. You just have to fear God—trust him, respect him, walk humbly with him.

That's the secret.

When life is confusing, fear God.

When things don't seem fair, fear God.

When you mess up, fear God.

When others mess up, fear God.

When you don't understand, fear God.

Not fear like terror—fear like reverence. Like awe. Like recognizing that God is God and you're not.

That's the posture that keeps you balanced. That's the foundation wisdom is built on.

WORKING WITH THE GRAIN

Remember the lumber at the beginning? The wise carpenter doesn't yell at the crooked board. They learn to work *with* the grain, not against it. That's what wisdom looks like in real life.

You stop demanding that everything be straight. You start trusting that God can make something beautiful even out of bent pieces. You accept your limits. You extend grace to others. You hold your plans loosely. You keep walking, even when you can't see the whole path.

And here's the surprising thing: When you stop fighting the crookedness and start trusting the Carpenter, you find a kind of peace you didn't know was possible. The world is bent. You're bent. But God isn't.

And he's still working.

9

WHY WON'T GOD JUST EXPLAIN EVERYTHING?

Remember when you were little and you asked "why" about everything?

"Why is the sky blue?"

"Why do dogs bark?"

"Why can't I stay up late?"

"Why? Why? Why?"

And eventually, after your parents tried really hard to explain, they hit that moment where they just said, "Sweetheart, that's just how it works." It wasn't that they didn't want to answer. Sometimes the answer was too complicated. Sometimes you weren't ready to understand. Sometimes there just wasn't a simple answer to give.

Here's the thing: We never really outgrow that. We still have "why" questions—they just get bigger.

Why do bad people sometimes win?

Why do good people sometimes suffer?

Why doesn't God stop evil right away?

Why does life feel so unfair?

And when we don't get answers, we feel the same frustration

we felt as kids: Why won't God just tell me? Ecclesiastes 8 is the Teacher's response to all of that. And his answer might surprise you.

YOU DON'T HAVE TO UNDERSTAND EVERYTHING

The chapter opens with a description of wisdom that's really beautiful: "Who is like the wise person, and who knows the interpretation of a matter? A person's wisdom brightens his face, and the sternness of his face is changed" (8:1).

Wisdom doesn't just make you smart. It makes you calm. It softens your face. It takes away that stressed, frustrated, clenched-jaw look that comes from trying to figure everything out.

Why? Because wisdom teaches you that you don't have to figure everything out. The wise person isn't calm because they have all the answers. They're calm because they trust the One who does.

DEALING WITH UNFAIR AUTHORITY

The next section talks about something that probably feels familiar: dealing with people who have power over you. "Keep the king's command. ... The one who keeps a command will not experience anything harmful, and a wise heart knows the right time and procedure" (8:2, 5). In the ancient world, kings had total power. You couldn't just disagree with them or walk out. If you made them mad, you could be punished—or worse.

The Teacher isn't saying kings are always right. He's saying: Be wise about how you handle authority. Sometimes the smartest thing to do is wait for the right moment instead of reacting right away.

This applies today too. You'll have teachers, coaches, bosses, and leaders who aren't always fair. Wisdom doesn't mean blindly obeying everything they say. But it also doesn't mean exploding every time something seems unfair. Wisdom waits. Wisdom picks the right time to speak up. Wisdom knows that patience often accomplishes more than anger.

YOU CAN'T CONTROL DEATH (OR ANYTHING ELSE)

Here's where it gets real: "No one has authority over the wind to restrain it, and there is no authority over the day of death" (8:8). You can't hold the wind. And you can't hold off death. No matter how healthy you eat, how careful you are, or how much you plan—eventually, everyone dies. You don't get to choose when.

The Teacher isn't being morbid. He's being honest. And his honesty has a purpose: Stop pretending you're in control.

We spend so much energy trying to control things we can't control—the future, other people, outcomes, circumstances. The Teacher says: Let it go. You're not in charge. God is. That's not scary. It's actually freeing. Because if God is in control, then you don't have to be.

WHEN BAD PEOPLE SEEM TO WIN

Now comes the part that really hurts: "I saw the wicked buried. They came and went from the holy place, and they were praised in the city where they did those things" (8:10).

The Teacher watched terrible people get honored. He saw wicked people show up at religious places, act spiritual, and then get praised by everyone when they died. Meanwhile, good people got ignored or mistreated.

Sound familiar? Maybe you've seen it too. The kid who cheats gets the better grade. The person who lies gets the promotion. The bully is popular, and the kind person gets overlooked.

It's infuriating.

And then the Teacher explains why evil seems to keep spreading: "Because the sentence against an evil act is not carried out quickly, the heart of people is filled with the desire to commit evil" (8:11). When people don't face consequences right away, they start thinking they can get away with anything. They assume God doesn't see. Or doesn't care. Or isn't going to do anything about it.

But here's what the Teacher says next—and it's one of the most important lines in the chapter: "Although a sinner does evil a hundred times and prolongs his life, I also know that it will go well with God-fearing people, for they are reverent before him" (8:12).

"I know." Not "I hope." Not "I wish." Not "Maybe."

I know.

Even when it doesn't look like it. Even when the wicked seem to be winning. Even when justice is delayed. The Teacher knows that in the end, things will go better for those who fear God. Justice may be slow. But it's not canceled.

WHEN LIFE FEELS BACKWARD

The Teacher gets even more honest: "There is a futility that is done on the earth: there are righteous people who get what the actions of the wicked deserve, and there are wicked people who get what the actions of the righteous deserve" (8:14).

Good people suffer. Bad people prosper. The world feels upside down. This is one of the hardest things about life. You expect that doing the right thing will lead to good results. But sometimes it doesn't. Sometimes it feels like the rules are broken.

The Teacher doesn't pretend this isn't real. He names it. He feels it. He calls it "meaningless"—vapor, mist, something that doesn't make sense.

But then—right after naming the unfairness—he says something unexpected: "So I commended enjoyment" (8:15).

Wait—what? Life is unfair and your response is... enjoy it?

Yes. Here's why.

JOY IS RESISTANCE

The Teacher isn't saying, "Pretend everything is fine." He's saying: Don't let the unfairness steal your joy. When life is hard and confusing, choosing to enjoy the good gifts God gives you is actually an act of faith. It's saying, "I don't understand everything, but I trust that God is still good." The Teacher ays, "Because there is nothing better for a person under the sun than to eat, drink, and enjoy himself, for this will accompany him in his labor during the days of his life that God gives him under the sun" (8:15).

Joy isn't pretending the bad stuff doesn't exist. Joy is refusing to let the bad stuff define your life. It's noticing the meal, the friendship, the sunshine, the small good things—even when the big picture is confusing.

That's holy stubbornness. That's what faith looks like when answers aren't coming.

YOU'LL NEVER FIGURE IT ALL OUT

The chapter ends with the Teacher admitting something important: "A person is unable to discover the work that is done under the sun. Even though a person labors hard to explore it, he cannot find it; even if a wise person claims to know it, he is unable to discover it" (8:17).

He tried. He studied, observed, analyzed, stayed up late thinking. And after all of it, he landed on this: "I can't fully understand what God is doing."

And that's okay. Not knowing isn't failure. It's being human. God's plans are bigger than our brains can handle. His timing is different from ours. His purposes stretch beyond what we can see. That's not a reason to give up. It's a reason to trust.

WHAT THIS MEANS FOR YOU

Ecclesiastes 8 doesn't give you neat answers to life's hardest questions. It gives you something better: a way to live when answers don't come.

Here's what the Teacher models:

Stay calm. Wisdom softens the face. Don't let confusion make you bitter or angry. Trust that God sees what you don't.

Be wise with authority. Not every battle needs to be fought right now. Timing matters. Patience matters.

Accept your limits. You can't control the future. You can't control death. You can't control outcomes. Let go of what isn't yours to hold.

Trust that justice is coming. Even when the wicked seem to win, God is not asleep. Delayed doesn't mean denied.

Choose joy anyway. Don't wait for life to be fair before you enjoy God's gifts. Eat. Laugh. Be grateful. That's not escapism—it's faith.

Stop demanding full explanations. You won't get them. Not because God doesn't care, but because his ways are bigger than yours. Trusting God is more important than understanding God.

THE KID IN THE BACK SEAT

Remember the kid asking "why" in the back seat? Eventually, that kid learns something: Even when they don't understand the route, the traffic, or the detours, they can trust the parent who's driving.

That's what Ecclesiastes 8 is teaching you. Life is confusing. Outcomes don't always make sense. Justice is delayed. The future is hidden. You don't have all the answers.

But God does. And he's driving. So sit back. Stay calm. Enjoy the ride where you can. And trust that even when the road makes no sense to you, the One behind the wheel knows exactly where he's going.

That's not giving up. That's wisdom. And wisdom, according to the Teacher, softens your face—because it frees you from having to figure out what only God can know.

10

NOBODY GETS OUT OF HERE ALIVE

You've probably been to a funeral, or at least heard about one. There's usually that one older guy who leans over, clears his throat, and says something like, "Well, none of us gets out of here alive." He thinks he's being clever—trying to lighten the mood. But what he doesn't realize is that he's basically quoting the Bible.

Because that's exactly what Ecclesiastes 9 is about.

Nobody escapes death. Nobody controls the future. Nobody can guarantee that their hard work will pay off the way they expect. Not the smartest person. Not the strongest. Not the most talented. Not even the most religious.

The Teacher has been building toward this point for the whole book. And in chapter 9, he finally says it straight: Life is fragile. You don't know what tomorrow holds. So live today like it matters.

THE YEARBOOK PROBLEM

Here's another way to think about it. You know how yearbooks have those "Most Likely to Succeed" awards? The star athlete.

The valedictorian. The student council president. Everyone expects them to take over the world.

Fast forward ten years.

The athlete blew out their knee and never played ball again. The "most likely to succeed" kid is working a random job they never planned on. Meanwhile, some quiet kid nobody noticed is running a successful business. The shy girl who barely talked in class is now saving lives as a nurse.

Life doesn't follow the script.

The Teacher puts it like this: "The race is not to the swift, or the battle to the strong, or bread to the wise, or riches to the discerning, or favor to the skillful; rather, time and chance happen to all of them" (9:11).

That's not saying talent doesn't matter. It does. But talent doesn't guarantee outcomes. Hard work doesn't guarantee results. You can do everything right and still not get what you expected.

Why? Because God is in control—not you. And God doesn't owe you a predictable life just because you followed all the rules. That's not scary. It's actually freeing. Because it means you can stop pretending you're in charge.

EVERYONE FACES THE SAME END

Here's where it gets heavy: "There is one fate for the righteous and the wicked, for the good and the bad. ... As it is for the good, so also it is for the sinner" (9:2–3). Death doesn't care if you're a good person. It doesn't care if you're rich or poor, famous or forgotten, religious or not. Everyone dies.

That feels unfair, right? Shouldn't the good people at least get more time? Shouldn't being righteous count for something?

The Teacher doesn't pretend this isn't frustrating. He calls it a "grievous evil"—something that's genuinely painful to accept. But he doesn't lie about it either.

Here's the thing: This doesn't mean being good is pointless. It means that being good isn't a life-extension plan. You don't do the right thing to avoid death. You do the right thing because it's right—and because God sees.

A LIVE DOG IS BETTER THAN A DEAD LION

Now here's a weird line that actually makes a lot of sense: "A live dog is better than a dead lion" (9:4). In the ancient world, dogs were considered gross—like street animals. Lions were majestic and powerful. But the Teacher says he'd rather be a living dog than a dead lion.

Why? Because the living still have something the dead don't: time. "For the living know that they will die, but the dead don't know anything. …There is no longer a portion for them in all that is done under the sun" (9:5–6). The dead are done. They can't love, work, learn, grow, repent, celebrate, or change. But the living? They still have a chance. Every breath is an opportunity. That's not depressing—it's motivating. You're still alive. You still have today. Don't waste it.

SO WHAT DO YOU DO?

Here's where the chapter takes a surprising turn. After all that heavy stuff about death and unpredictability, you might expect the Teacher to say, "So just give up." But he doesn't. Instead, he says: "Go, eat your bread with pleasure, and drink your wine with a cheerful heart, for God has already accepted your works" (9:7).

Wait—go be happy?

Yes. That's the command. Not "mope around." Not "stress about the future." Not "worry about things you can't control." Eat with joy. Drink with a happy heart. Enjoy your life.

Why? Because God gave you this day. He gave you food, friends, family, breath. And he approves of you enjoying those gifts. Joy isn't a distraction from the spiritual life—it *is* the spiritual life when it's rooted in gratitude.

WHITE CLOTHES AND OIL

The Teacher uses some ancient imagery that might sound weird to us: "Let your clothes be white all the time, and never let oil be lacking on your head" (9:8). In those days, white clothes were for celebrations. Oil was for festive occasions.

The Teacher is saying: Don't dress your soul in funeral clothes all the time. Wear joy when you can. Celebrate when there's something to celebrate.

That doesn't mean pretend everything is fine when it's not. But it does mean: Don't let life's hardships steal every good moment. Choose to notice the gifts.

LOVE THE PEOPLE IN FRONT OF YOU

Here's one of the most personal lines in the chapter: "Enjoy life with the wife you love all the days of your fleeting life, which has been given to you under the sun, all your fleeting days. For that is your portion in life" (9:9). Life is short. Life is vapor. But that doesn't make it worthless—it makes it precious.

The Teacher is saying: Love the people in front of you. Don't wait until you've "made it" to appreciate your relationships.

Don't put off connection until life calms down. Treasure the people God has put in your life *now*.

Because time runs out.

WORK LIKE IT MATTERS

Next comes a call to action: "Whatever your hands find to do, do with all your strength, because there is no work, planning, knowledge, or wisdom in [the grave] where you are going" (9:10). When you're dead, you can't work, plan, learn, or grow. So do those things now—with everything you've got.

This isn't about being stressed or overworked. It's about being present. Engaged. Fully alive.

Don't sleepwalk through life. Don't half-do your work. Don't coast through your relationships. You've got a limited amount of time—use it well.

YOU CAN'T PREDICT THE FUTURE

The Teacher circles back to one of his main themes: "Again I saw under the sun that the race is not to the swift, or the battle to the strong; … rather, time and chance happen to all of them" (9:11). You can't guarantee outcomes. The fastest runner might trip. The smartest student might bomb the test. The best plan might fall apart.

That's not meant to make you give up. It's meant to keep you humble. Don't put all your hope in your own abilities. Trust God with the results.

Then comes a sobering image: "For certainly no one knows his time: like fish caught in a cruel net or like birds caught in a trap, so people are trapped in an evil time as it suddenly falls on them" (9:12). Fish don't know when the net is coming. Birds don't know when the trap will snap. And neither do we. Hard times come without warning. Death arrives on its own schedule.

That's not meant to terrify you. It's meant to focus you. Stop assuming you've got endless time. Live today like it matters—because it does.

WHAT THIS MEANS FOR YOU

Ecclesiastes 9 is one of the most honest and most hopeful chapters in the whole book. Here's what it's teaching:

You're not in control. You can't predict the future. You can't guarantee outcomes. You can't escape death. So stop pretending otherwise.

But you're still alive. And that means you still have today. You still have opportunities. You still have time to love, work, grow, and enjoy.

Joy is obedience. God wants you to enjoy the gifts he gives. Eating with gladness, celebrating good things, treasuring relationships—that's not selfish. That's worship.

Work with your whole heart. Don't coast. Don't half-live. Whatever you do, do it fully. Because one day, the chance to do it will be gone.

Trust God with the results. You can't control outcomes, but God can. Do your best, then let go. He sees. He knows. He's got it.

THE FREEDOM OF NOT BEING IN CHARGE

Here's the bottom line. Most people spend their lives trying to control things they can't control—the future, other people, outcomes, success, even death. And it exhausts them.

The Teacher says: let it go. You don't have to figure out tomorrow. You just have to be faithful today. You don't have to guarantee success. You just have to work with integrity. You don't have to understand God's whole plan. You just have to trust that he has one.

That's freedom. Real freedom.

So eat your food with joy. Love the people in front of you. Work hard at whatever's in your hands. And stop pretending you're in the driver's seat.

God's driving. And he knows the way.

None of us gets out of here alive—but that's exactly why every moment matters.

So live like it.

11

DEAD FLIES &
QUIET HEROES

There's a story carpenters like to tell. A master craftsman spent his whole career building beautiful homes. His work was perfect—clean joints, straight angles, the kind of quality everyone admired. One day, right before finishing a nearly flawless project, he accidentally left a small pencil mark on a wooden beam. It was tiny. Barely noticeable.

But he couldn't unsee it.

For years afterward, every time he drove past that house, all he could remember was that little mark. Not the beautiful trim. Not the hours of careful work. Not the fact that the house was basically perfect. Just the one small flaw. He used to say, "A house remembers the mistakes louder than the craftsmanship."

Ecclesiastes 9–10 would totally agree. The Teacher opens this section with one of the most vivid images in the whole book: "Dead flies make a perfumer's oil ferment and stink; so a little folly outweighs wisdom and honor" (10:1).

One tiny mistake can wreck something beautiful. A few dead flies can ruin an expensive bottle of perfume. A careless word can destroy a friendship. A moment of impatience can unravel a reputation you spent years building.

It's easy to remember the fly. It's harder to remember the fragrance.

THE HERO NOBODY REMEMBERED

Before getting into all the ways foolishness messes things up, the Teacher tells a story about wisdom: "There was a small city with few men in it. A great king came against it, surrounded it, and built large siege works against it. Now a poor wise man was found in the city, and he delivered the city by his wisdom" (9:14–15).

Picture this: A massive army shows up outside a tiny, defenseless town. Everyone inside is terrified. There's no way they can fight back. They're doomed.

But then a poor wise man—nobody special, no title, no power—figures out a way to save them. Maybe he negotiated with the king. Maybe he came up with a clever strategy. The Bible doesn't tell us how. It just says his wisdom delivered the city.

Sounds like a hero story, right? But here's the painful part: "Yet no one remembered that poor man" (9:15). He saved everyone. And they forgot him.

That's what wisdom is often like. It works quietly. It doesn't make a lot of noise. And when the crisis passes, people forget who helped them.

But the Teacher still says: "Wisdom is better than strength" (9:16). Even when it's overlooked. Even when it doesn't get applause. Wisdom still matters more than power.

QUIET WORDS BEAT LOUD FOOLS

Here's another line worth remembering: "The calm words of the wise are heeded more than the shouts of a ruler over fools" (9:17). In our world, loud people get attention. The person who yells the most, posts the most, argues the most—they seem like they're in charge. But the Teacher says that's not real authority. Volume isn't the same as wisdom.

A wise person doesn't need to scream. Their words carry weight because they're true—not because they're loud. Meanwhile, fools shout because they've got nothing real to say. They turn up the volume to cover up the emptiness.

THE FOOL'S GIVEAWAY

The Teacher gets kind of funny here: "Even when the fool walks along the road, his heart lacks sense, and he shows everyone he is a fool" (10:3). You don't have to ask if someone is foolish. Just watch them. The way they walk, talk, react—it all gives them away.

Foolishness is loud. It can't help but advertise itself.

Wisdom, on the other hand, is quiet. It doesn't brag. It doesn't need to.

WHEN THE BOSS GETS MAD

Here's some practical wisdom: "If the ruler's anger rises against you, don't leave your post, for calmness puts great offenses to rest" (10:4). Ever had someone in authority—a teacher, a coach, a parent—get mad at you? The natural reaction is to either blow up back at them or run away.

The Teacher says: Stay calm. Don't panic. Don't fight. Don't flee. Just be steady. A peaceful response can often defuse a tense situation better than arguing or running. That doesn't mean you're a pushover. It means you're wise enough not to make things worse.

SHARPEN THE AXE FIRST

Here's one of the most practical verses in the whole book: "If the ax is dull, and one does not sharpen its edge, then one must exert more strength; however, the advantage of wisdom is that it brings success" (10:10). A dull axe makes you work harder. A sharp axe makes the job easier.

A fool just swings harder, wears themselves out, and wonders why nothing's working. A wise person stops, sharpens the blade, and then works smarter. This applies to everything. Before you rush into a project, a conversation, or a decision—take time to prepare. Sharpen the blade. Think before you act.

THE FOOL'S MOUTH

The Teacher has a lot to say about talking too much: "The words from the mouth of a wise person are gracious, but the lips of a fool consume him. The beginning of the words from his mouth is folly, but the end of his speaking is evil madness; yet the fool multiplies words" (10:12–14).

Fools talk too much. And the more they talk, the dumber they sound. They start with something kind of silly, and by the time they're done, they've said something completely crazy.

Meanwhile, the wise speak graciously. Their words build people up. They don't need to fill every silence with noise.

Here's a simple test: If you're talking more than you're listening, you might be heading in the wrong direction.

THE FOOL WHO CAN'T FIND THE CITY

This one is kind of hilarious: "The struggles of fools weary them, for they don't know how to go to the city" (10:15). In the ancient world, the road to town was obvious. Everyone knew it. You couldn't miss it. But the Teacher imagines a fool so confused, so disorganized, so wrapped up in their own chaos, that they can't even find the easy path.

The point? Foolishness makes simple things complicated. Wisdom makes complicated things simple.

WHEN LEADERS ARE FOOLS

Now the Teacher turns to something bigger: what happens when fools are in charge. "How terrible it is for a country whose king is a child and whose leaders eat all morning" (10:16). A child king here means an immature king. Someone who acts like a child instead of a responsible adult. And to "eat all morning" means leaders who party instead of doing their job.

When people in charge are foolish, everyone suffers. The country falls apart. Things stop working. Problems pile up while the leaders are busy having fun.

But then the Teacher gives the opposite picture: "Blessed are you, land, when your king is a son of nobles and your princes feast at the proper time— for strength and not for drunkenness" (10:17). Good leaders know the right time for celebration and the right time for work. They eat to refuel for service, not to escape their responsibilities.

LAZY LEADERS, LEAKY ROOFS

Here's another image: "Because of laziness the roof caves in, and because of negligent hands the house leaks" (10:18). When leaders—or anyone, really—stop doing their job, things fall apart. The roof sags. The house leaks. What used to be solid starts crumbling. Neglect is quiet, but it's deadly. If you ignore something long enough, it will collapse.

WATCH YOUR WORDS (EVEN IN PRIVATE)

The chapter ends with a warning that might sound funny, but it's serious: "Do not curse the king even in your thoughts, and do not curse a rich person even in your bedroom, for a bird of the sky may carry the message, and a winged creature may report the matter" (10:20). Ever heard the phrase, "A little bird told me"? It comes from this verse.

The Teacher is saying: Be careful what you say, even in private. Words escape. Secrets leak. That thing you mumbled under your breath might get back to the wrong person.

This isn't about being fake or never having opinions. It's about being wise with your words. Don't say something in private that you'd be embarrassed to say in public.

WHAT THIS MEANS FOR YOU

Ecclesiastes 9–10 is basically a guidebook for living wisely in a world full of foolishness. Here's what to take away:

Small things matter. A few dead flies can ruin perfume. A single careless moment can undo years of good work. Pay attention to the little stuff.

Wisdom often goes unnoticed. The poor wise man saved a whole city and nobody remembered him. Don't expect applause for doing the right thing. Do it anyway.

Quiet beats loud. The world rewards noise, but wisdom speaks softly. You don't have to be the loudest person in the room to have the most impact.

Stay calm under pressure. When someone in authority blows up, don't panic. Calmness disarms conflict.

Sharpen the axe. Preparation beats raw effort. Work smart, not just hard.

Talk less. Fools multiply words. The wise know when to be quiet.

Take responsibility. Laziness leads to leaky roofs—literally and metaphorically. Do your job. Don't let things fall apart because you didn't feel like showing up.

Guard your words. Even private complaints have a way of getting out. Speak carefully.

DEAD FLIES AND LASTING FRAGRANCE

Here's the bottom line. It's easy to mess things up. One careless word, one lazy decision, one small compromise—and something beautiful is ruined. Dead flies always float to the top.

But it's also possible to live wisely. To build something good, even if nobody notices. To speak carefully. To work diligently. To stay calm when others panic. To be the quiet person whose wisdom blesses everyone around them.

The world might forget you. But God won't.

And in the end, the fragrance of a wise life lasts longer than the stench of a thousand foolish mistakes.

So sharpen your axe. Watch your words. Pay attention to the small things.

And don't let the flies ruin the perfume.

12

JUST JUMP

Have you ever stood on a diving board? You climb the ladder. You walk out to the edge. You look down at the water—which suddenly seems a lot farther away than it did from the ground. Your friends are cheering. The lifeguard is watching. And your legs... your legs have decided they'd rather stay right where they are. Everything inside you screams, "Just jump!"

But the longer you stand there, the harder it gets. You start worrying about your form. The splash. The angle. Whether the water is cold. Whether everyone is laughing at you. Whether you'll somehow mess this up in a way that will haunt you forever.

Here's the thing about diving boards: The longer you wait, the less likely you are to jump. Most of us eventually fell in by accident because our legs gave out—dignity first, body second.

Ecclesiastes 11 is basically the Teacher yelling, "Stop over-thinking! Just jump!"

CAST YOUR BREAD ON THE WATER

The chapter opens with one of the weirdest-sounding lines in the whole Bible: "Cast your bread upon the waters, for you will find it after many days" (11:1). What does that even mean?

In the ancient world, "casting bread on the waters" could mean a couple of things. Merchants would load ships with goods and send them across the sea—not knowing if storms, pirates, or bad markets would swallow everything. Farmers in flooded areas would scatter seed into the water, trusting that it would land in good soil when the waters went down.

Either way, the point is the same: Take the risk. You can't wait until you're 100% sure everything will work out. You can't demand guarantees before you act. Sometimes you just have to throw the bread and trust that God will bring something back.

STOP WAITING FOR PERFECT CONDITIONS

Here's where the Teacher gets really practical: "Whoever watches the wind will not plant; whoever looks at the clouds will not reap" (11:4). In farming, you have to plant at the right time or you won't get a harvest. But if you spend all your time obsessing over the weather—waiting for the perfect day with no wind and no clouds—you'll never plant anything. And if you never plant, you'll never harvest.

The same is true in life. Some people never start because they're waiting for the perfect moment:

- The perfect amount of money
- The perfect amount of confidence
- The perfect circumstances
- The perfect feeling that everything will work out

Guess what? That moment never comes.

The Teacher is saying: Stop waiting. The conditions will never be perfect. The weather will never be exactly right. You'll never have all the information you want. At some point, you just have to plant the seed and trust God with the results.

YOU DON'T KNOW—AND THAT'S OKAY

Here's one of the most important ideas in this chapter: "As you do not know the path of the wind, or how the body is formed in a mother's womb, so you cannot understand the work of God, the Maker of all things" (11:5).

You don't know how the wind moves. You don't know how a baby grows inside a mother. There's so much about God's work that's completely beyond your understanding. And the Teacher says that's fine. We tend to treat not knowing as a problem. Like if we could just figure everything out, then we'd be ready to act.

But the Teacher flips that around. He says your ignorance isn't a bug—it's a feature. You're not supposed to have it all figured out. You're not God. You don't see the whole picture. And that's actually freeing. Because if you don't have to understand everything before you act, then you can stop stressing about having all the answers. You can just do the next right thing and trust God with the outcome.

SPREAD IT AROUND

Here's another piece of wisdom: "Invest in seven ventures, yes, in eight; you do not know what disaster may come upon the land" (11:2).

The Teacher is saying: Don't put all your eggs in one basket. Spread your efforts around. Be generous in multiple ways. Help multiple people. Try multiple things. Because you don't know what's going to work and what isn't. You don't know what disaster might wipe out one area of your life. This isn't about being paranoid. It's about being wise. The future is uncertain, so don't stake everything on one outcome.

But there's another layer here too. This isn't just about protecting yourself—it's about being generous. Give freely. Share what you have. Help people when you can. Because you never know when you might be the one who needs help.

Generous people aren't generous because they have everything figured out. They're generous because they trust that God is the real Provider—not them.

SOW IN THE MORNING AND EVENING

Here's the Teacher's final push: "Sow your seed in the morning and at evening let your hands not be idle, for you do not know which will succeed, whether this or that, or whether both will do equally well" (11:6).

Don't just plant once and wait. Keep planting. Keep working. Keep trying. Morning and evening. Early and late. Again and again.

Why? Because you don't know which effort will succeed. Maybe the morning seed will grow. Maybe the evening seed will. Maybe both. Maybe neither. You can't control that. But you can control whether you keep showing up.

The person who only plants once and then sits around waiting for results is going to be disappointed. The person who keeps planting, keeps working, keeps being faithful—they're the ones who eventually see a harvest.

WHAT THIS MEANS FOR YOU

Ecclesiastes 11:1–6 is one of the most encouraging sections in the whole book. After all the heavy stuff about death and injustice and things we can't control, the Teacher finally says: So get moving! Here's what he's teaching:

Stop waiting for perfect conditions. They're not coming. The weather will never be exactly right. You'll never feel fully ready. At some point, you just have to start.

Take faithful risks. Casting bread on the water isn't reckless—it's trusting God with the outcome. You do your part; God handles the results.

You don't have to understand everything. You're not supposed to know how it all works. That's God's job. Your job is to be faithful with what's in front of you.

Be generous. Share what you have. Help where you can. Don't hoard out of fear. Trust that God will provide.

Keep planting. Morning and evening. Again and again. You don't know which effort will succeed, so keep showing up.

THE FREEDOM OF NOT KNOWING

Here's the surprising twist in all of this. Most people think uncertainty is the enemy. They want guarantees. They want to know exactly what's going to happen before they commit to anything.

But the Teacher says uncertainty is actually freeing. Think about it. If you had to know the outcome before you acted, you'd never do anything. You'd be paralyzed forever, waiting for information you'll never have.

But if you trust that God is in control—if you believe he's the one who makes seeds grow and babies form and the future unfold—then you don't need guarantees. You can act in faith. You can take risks. You can be generous. You can plant seeds without knowing which ones will sprout.

Uncertainty isn't a problem to solve. It's an invitation to trust.

BACK TO THE DIVING BOARD

Remember the diving board? Eventually, you jump. Maybe not gracefully. Maybe not confidently. But you jump.

And you know what? The water will be fine. You won't die. You won't even really embarrass yourself. And afterward, you probably will climb right back up and do it again.

That's what the Teacher is inviting you to do in Ecclesiastes 11. Stop standing on the edge, calculating every angle, waiting for the perfect moment. Stop letting fear freeze you in place.

Just jump.

Not because you have all the answers. Not because you know exactly how it's going to turn out. But because God is in the water. God is in the outcome. God is in the future you can't see.

Your job isn't to figure everything out. Your job is to be faithful.

Cast your bread. Plant your seed. Share what you have. Keep working.

And trust the God who knows what you don't.

That's not recklessness. That's faith.

And faith, according to the Teacher, is the only way to actually live.

So stop waiting.

Jump.

13

GETTING OFF THE LADDER

A while back, I visited an older man from my church—let's call him Mr. Williams. He had just decided to stop driving. Nobody made him do it. He hadn't been in an accident. His kids didn't take his keys away. He just looked at me and said, "I can still drive. I just can't bounce back from the surprises anymore." That might be one of the most honest sentences I've ever heard.

He wasn't bitter about it. He wasn't complaining. He was just being realistic. "When I was young," he said, "the world felt like it was waiting for me. Now it feels like it's lapping me."

That's what getting older is like. The curbs look taller. The steps seem steeper. The nights feel darker. The world moves a little faster than your legs can keep up with.

Ecclesiastes 11–12 are about exactly that—the sweetness of life, the reality of aging, and why it all matters to God.

LIGHT IS SWEET

The chapter starts with something beautiful: "Light is sweet, and it pleases the eyes to see the sun" (11:7). After all the heavy stuff in Ecclesiastes—injustice, death, things we can't control—suddenly the Teacher just... appreciates being alive. He's not pretending life is easy. He's just saying: Waking up to see the sun is a gift. Being alive is a gift. Every day you get is grace.

The word "sweet" here means something you actually taste and enjoy—not just something you acknowledge. The Teacher wants us to savor life, not just survive it.

DON'T FORGET THE HARD DAYS

But right after that, he adds: "However many years anyone may live, let them enjoy them all. But let them also remember the days of darkness, for there will be many" (11:8).

Life isn't all sunshine. There will be hard days. Lots of them. The Teacher isn't trying to bum you out. He's trying to help you be realistic. If you only expect good things, you'll be crushed when hard things come. But if you remember that darkness is part of life, you can still enjoy the light without being shocked when it fades.

This is wisdom. Hold joy and grief together. Don't pretend everything is fine when it isn't. But don't let the hard stuff steal your ability to appreciate the good stuff either.

A MESSAGE TO YOUNG PEOPLE

Here's where it gets personal: "Be happy, young man, while you are young, and let your heart give you joy in the days of your youth. Follow the ways of your heart and whatever your eyes see" (11:9). Wait—is the Teacher telling young people to just do whatever they want? Not exactly. He's saying: Enjoy your youth. You have energy, curiosity, strength, and opportunities you won't always have. That's a gift from God. Don't waste it being miserable.

But then he adds the guardrail: "But know that for all these things God will bring you into judgment." In other words: You're free to enjoy life, but you're not free from responsibility. God sees how you use your youth. Joy without wisdom is dangerous. Freedom without reverence leads to disaster. The Teacher isn't saying, "Have fun but feel guilty about it." He's saying: Enjoy life wisely. Let your joy be guided by the fear of God, not just by whatever feels good in the moment.

DON'T WASTE YOUR YOUTH

Here's another important line: "So then, banish anxiety from your heart and cast off the troubles of your body, for youth and vigor are meaningless" (11:10). "Meaningless" here means "temporary"—like vapor, like mist. Youth doesn't last. Your energy won't stay at this level forever. Your strength won't always be there.

So don't waste your youth being bitter, anxious, or angry. Don't spend your best years chasing things that will wreck you later. And don't assume you have forever. Youth is like a sunrise—beautiful, but brief. Enjoy it while it's here.

REMEMBER YOUR CREATOR

Now comes one of the most famous lines in the whole book: "Remember your Creator in the days of your youth, before the days of trouble come and the years approach when you will say, 'I find no pleasure in them'" (12:1). The Teacher is telling you: Don't wait until you're old to start following God.

Why? Because the habits you build now shape who you become later. If you learn to trust God when you're young, that trust will carry you through the hard stuff ahead. If you wait until life falls apart to start paying attention to God, it'll be a lot harder.

"Remember" here doesn't just mean "think about." It means "orient your whole life around." Make God the center now—before the hard days come.

A POEM ABOUT GETTING OLD

What comes next is one of the most poetic—and kind of sad— parts of the Bible. The Teacher describes what it's like to get old using a bunch of metaphors. It's like watching a beautiful house slowly fall apart. "Before the sun and the light and the moon and the stars grow dark, and the clouds return after the rain..." (12:2). Life gets darker. Recovery takes longer. Storms don't pass as quickly as they used to.

Then he describes the body breaking down:

- "When the keepers of the house tremble..." The arms and hands start shaking.
- "When the strong men stoop..." The legs and back get weak.
- "When the grinders cease because they are few..." Teeth fall out.
- "When those looking through the windows grow dim..." Eyes stop working well.

It keeps going:

- "When the doors to the street are closed..." The mouth stays shut because chewing is hard.
- "When people rise up at the sound of birds..." Sleep becomes light; you wake up at the smallest noise.
- "When the almond tree blossoms..." Hair turns white.
- "When the grasshopper drags itself along..." Moving becomes slow and painful.
- "When desire no longer is stirred..." Appetite fades.

The Teacher isn't making fun of old people. He's honoring them by telling the truth. Aging is hard. Bodies break down. Things that used to be easy become difficult.

But he's also warning the young: This is coming for you too. Don't act like you'll be strong forever.

THE END OF THE ROAD

The poem ends with death: "Remember him—before the silver cord is severed, and the golden bowl is broken; before the pitcher is shattered at the spring, and the wheel broken at the well" (12:6). These are all images of things that suddenly break. A lamp crashes. A pitcher shatters. A well stops working. That's what death is like. One moment you're here; the next moment, you're not.

And then the final line: "The dust returns to the ground it came from, and the spirit returns to God who gave it" (12:7). We came from dust, and we go back to dust. Our bodies return to the earth. But our spirits? They return to God—the one who breathed life into us in the first place. That's not depressing. That's reality. And it's also hope. Death isn't the end of everything. God receives us back.

ALL IS VAPOR—BUT THAT'S NOT BAD NEWS

The Teacher closes this section with the same line he started the whole book with: "'Meaningless! Meaningless!' says the Teacher. 'Everything is meaningless!'" (12:8). By now, you know what that word means. It's *hebel*—vapor, mist, breath. Life is temporary. It slips through your fingers. You can't hold onto it.

But here's the important part: That's not a reason to give up. That's a reason to pay attention. If life were permanent, we'd take it for granted. But because it's short, every moment matters. Because it's fragile, every day is a gift. Because it doesn't last, we need to remember the One who does.

WHAT THIS MEANS FOR YOU

Ecclesiastes 11–12 is the Teacher's final message before wrapping up the book. And here's what he wants you to know:

Life is sweet—enjoy it. Don't wait until some future moment to appreciate what you have. The sun is shining now. Savor it.

Youth doesn't last—use it wisely. You have energy, strength, and opportunities that won't always be there. Don't waste them on bitterness, anxiety, or foolish choices.

Remember your Creator now. Don't wait until you're old to start following God. Build the habits of faith while you're young, and they'll carry you through the hard days ahead.

Aging is real—respect it. Your body will break down someday. It's just the way things are. Honor the elderly. Prepare for your own future. And don't assume you're invincible.

Death is certain—but God holds your spirit. This life ends, but God doesn't. The dust returns to the earth, and the spirit returns to him. That's not the end of the story. It's the beginning of something bigger.

MR. WILLIAMS, ONE MORE TIME

Remember Mr. Williams? The guy who gave up his car keys? He said one more thing that day that stuck with me. "I used to think slowing down was punishment. Now I think it's mercy. It forces me to pay attention to things I used to rush past."

That's the wisdom of Ecclesiastes. Youth teaches you to run. Age teaches you to notice. And God uses both to teach you to remember.

So don't wait until life slows down to start paying attention. Remember your Creator now. Enjoy the light while it's sweet. Use your strength while you have it. And trust that the God who gave you breath will receive you when that breath is done.

That's not a sad ending.

That's the only way to really live.

14

THE ONLY THING THAT MATTERS

In a small-town hardware store, tucked between the plumbing aisle and a dusty display of rakes, there was a bulletin board. The sign at the top said, "Advice from the Regulars." It started years ago when the store owner got tired of answering the same questions every spring. So he scribbled a note and tacked it up: "If you don't know what you're doing, ask someone who does. If you think you know what you're doing, ask twice." People thought it was funny. But they also took it seriously.

Over time, the board filled up. Customers scribbled bits of wisdom on receipts, scrap paper, even cardboard. Some advice was practical:

- "Measure twice, cut once."
- "If the pipe hisses, don't tap it—run."
- "Never tighten anything you may need to loosen later."

Other notes were deeper:

- "Pride builds ladders too tall to climb down safely."

- "If everyone else is the problem, you might be."
- "Experience is a teacher with sharp elbows."

Visitors from out of town thought it was just a quirky decoration. But the locals knew better. More than once, someone facing a tough decision stood in front of that board, reading quietly. One of the regulars once said, "Every line on that board cost somebody something."

One day, a teenager wandered up to the bulletin board holding a package of wood screws. He looked totally confused. After a minute, an older man walked over. The boy handed him the screws and asked, "Do I need these?"

The man squinted at the box and said, "Son, what are you trying to do?"

The kid shrugged. If he knew that, he wouldn't be standing there.

The man chuckled, walked him back to the lumber section, and said, "Let's start with the basics. If you don't know your goal, every aisle looks right."

That line could have been written straight into Ecclesiastes.

THE END OF THE BOOK

Ecclesiastes 12:9–14 is the conclusion of the whole book. After everything the Teacher has said—about life being vapor, about death being certain, about joy and suffering and wisdom and limits—now someone else steps in to wrap things up. It's like the narrator of the book putting his hand on your shoulder and saying, "Okay, let's make sure you got the point."

And the point is surprisingly simple.

THE TEACHER CARED ABOUT YOU

The narrator of Ecclesiastes starts by honoring the Teacher: "Not only was the Teacher wise, but he also imparted knowledge to the people. He pondered and searched out and set in order many proverbs. The Teacher searched to find just the right words, and what he wrote was upright and true" (12:9–10).

The Teacher wasn't just smart. He was generous. He didn't keep his wisdom to himself—he "imparted knowledge to the people." He worked hard to find the right words. He cared about truth and about making it beautiful.

That's what good teachers do. They don't just dump information on you. They think carefully about how to say things so they actually land. They want to help, not just impress.

The Teacher spent his whole life figuring out how the world works. And then he shared what he learned—not to show off, but to help people like you live well.

GOADS AND NAILS

Here's one of the coolest verses in the whole book: "The words of the wise are like goads, their collected sayings like firmly embedded nails—given by one Shepherd" (12:11). Two images here: goads and nails.

Goads were sharp sticks used by shepherds to poke animals and get them moving in the right direction. They weren't meant to hurt—they were meant to nudge. That's what wisdom does sometimes. It pokes you. It stings a little. It says, "Hey, you're going the wrong way."

Nails are the opposite. They hold things together. They anchor structures so they don't fall apart. Wisdom does that too.

It gives you something solid to hang your decisions on.

So wisdom both prods you forward and anchors you down. It moves you and steadies you at the same time. And here's the really important part: both come from "one Shepherd." Capital S. That's God.

The Teacher wasn't making stuff up. His wisdom came from the same God who made the world. When Ecclesiastes challenges you, that's God nudging you. When it gives you something solid to stand on, that's God anchoring you.

A WARNING ABOUT BOOKS

Next comes a funny line: "Be warned, my son, of anything in addition to them. Of making many books there is no end, and much study wearies the body" (12:12). Is the Bible telling you not to read? Not exactly.

The narrator is saying: Don't get lost in endless searching. There will always be another book, another theory, another idea. You can spend your whole life chasing knowledge and never actually live.

This isn't anti-learning. The Teacher was obviously super smart and studied a lot. But he's warning against using learning as an excuse to avoid obedience. Some people read a hundred books about life but never actually follow God. They're always studying, never doing. At some point, you have to stop gathering information and start trusting God.

THE WHOLE POINT

Now comes the climax—the single most important verse in the whole book: "Now all has been heard; here is the conclusion of the matter: Fear God and keep his commandments, for this is the duty of all mankind" (12:13). That's it. That's the whole book in one sentence.

Fear God. Not terror—reverence. Respect. Awe. Recognizing that God is God and you're not. Letting that reality shape everything about how you live.

Keep his commandments. Obey what God says. Not to earn his love—you already have that. But because his instructions are good. Because he knows how life works. Because following him is the path to real life. The Hebrew actually says, "This is the whole of man." In other words, this is what being human is all about. This is why you exist. This is the center of everything.

After twelve chapters of wrestling with hard questions—Why do good people suffer? Why does life feel meaningless? Why can't we control our futures?—the answer is shockingly simple. Fear God. Keep his commandments. That's everything.

JUDGMENT IS COMING

The book ends with one final truth: "For God will bring every deed into judgment, including every hidden thing, whether it is good or evil" (12:14). That might sound scary. But it's actually really hopeful.

Remember how the Teacher kept noticing that life isn't fair? Good people suffer. Bad people prosper. Things don't work out the way they should. This verse says: That's not the end of the story. God sees everything. Even the hidden stuff. Even the things nobody noticed. And one day, he's going to set it all right.

The wicked won't get away with it forever. The righteous won't be forgotten. Every quiet act of faithfulness, every private sacrifice, every time you did the right thing when nobody was watching—God saw. And it matters.

Judgment isn't just about punishment. It's about justice. It's the promise that your life counts. That right and wrong actually matter. That the chaos you see now isn't the final word.

WHAT THIS MEANS FOR YOU

Ecclesiastes has taken us on a wild ride. Life is vapor. Death is certain. We can't control the future. We can't figure everything out. A lot of what we chase doesn't satisfy. But here's what the book has been building toward the whole time:

God is real. In a world full of vapor, he's the only solid thing.

Your life matters. Not because you'll be famous or rich or successful, but because God sees you and will judge everything you do.

Reverence and obedience are the whole point. You don't need a hundred philosophies. You don't need to figure out every mystery. You just need to fear God and follow him.

That's it. That's the conclusion.

BACK TO THE HARDWARE STORE

Remember the teenager with the wood screws? He walked into the store thinking he needed screws. But what he really needed was direction. He didn't know what he was trying to build, so every aisle looked right—and wrong at the same time. The older man didn't hand him a catalog of every possible tool. He didn't lecture him on carpentry theory. He just said, "Let's start with the basics."

That's what Ecclesiastes does. After all the questions, after all the wrestling, after all the honest observations about how confusing life can be—the book puts a hand on your shoulder and says: "Let's start with the basics." Fear God. Keep his commandments. Everything else hangs on those nails.

VICTORY IN THE VAPOR

Ecclesiastes started with "Meaningless! Meaningless! Everything is meaningless!" It ends with "Fear God and keep his commandments." That's not a contradiction. It's a journey.

Life really is like vapor—short, unpredictable, impossible to hold. But God isn't. He's solid. He's eternal. He sees everything. And he's the one who gives meaning to the mist.

You can't control the future. But you can trust the One who does.

You can't figure out every mystery. But you can worship the God who knows them all.

You can't make life last forever. But you can live it in a way that echoes into eternity.

The book that began in fog ends in clarity. The journey that started with confusion ends with calling.

Fear God. Keep his commandments.

That's the whole of being human.

And that's enough.